Endorsements

' … I love Jacky's books!' – **Melissa Porter, TV presenter**

'Jacky's writing has inspired me in so many ways. She is and always will be an Angel in my eyes.' – **Barrie John, TV's Psychic Medium**

'… Jacky Newcomb's books have made her a well-respected name in the study of angels and afterlife communication. Jacky's work is essential reading for anyone interested in learning more about this fascinating subject …'
– **Uri Geller, www.urigeller.com**

'My mind has always been open to life beyond this life … if yours isn't, read Jacky Newcomb's books … and if it is … just enjoy!' – **Suzi Quatro, musician, singer/songwriter, actor, author, TV and radio presenter**

'… Whenever I meet people in the course of my work [who are] interested in angels, I point them in Jacky's direction – she is the fountain of all "angel" knowledge. I know her books have helped so many.'
– **Tony Stockwell, TV's Psychic Medium and bestselling author**

'If you want to know anything about angels, then Jacky Newcomb's books are a great place to start; they always make me smile with such inspiring and uplifting true-life tales of angelic encounters. Jacky has been researching this subject for many years so knows her stuff; she is truly passionate about angels!'
– **Katy Evans, editor *Soul & Spirit* magazine**

'Jacky writes inspirational books and articles about angels, all from the heart, spiritual and enlightening …' – ***Woman's Weekly***

'… Jacky Newcomb has established a reputation as one of the country's leading paranormal experiences experts …' – ***Staffordshire Life* magazine**

'No matter what your beliefs are, you can't help but feel hope that there is something beyond the certainty of death. Personally, I felt deeply touched by a number of the stories in Jacky's book and I felt reassured and calmed by her approach in relaying these messages from beyond! The book itself, like the lady, is approachable and friendly.' – **Marion Davies, Managing Director, *SimplyHealth247* magazine**

'First of all, cancel out all notions of veils, crystal balls, and associated ghostly, pantomime-style antics. Contrary to popular misconceptions, Jacky Newcomb is a non-cloa[k] [...] wn admission, leads wha[t] [...] **magazine**

'... Jacky Newcomb has helped save many lives. Young and old, male and female, black and white, Jacky has been instrumental in helping thousands of people throughout the world understand and deal with questions regarding the afterlife...' – *Our Time* **magazine**

'Jacky Newcomb is the Angel Lady, offering hope and enchantment to those wishing to connect with angels, and comfort and solace to those dealing with loss. Her books are entertaining, engrossing and filled with incredible stories of real-life angelic encounters.' – **Tania Ahsan, editor, *Kindred Spirit***

'You know you can trust Jacky ... Jacky is simply inspirational.' – **Mary Bryce, editor, *Chat – it's fate***

'Jacky doesn't simply write about angels and other esoteric topics, she brings them to life in a magical, memorable way.' – **Sue Ricketts, editor, *Fate and Fortune* magazine**

'... Jacky's a fascinating lady ... and very down to earth ... she's an Angel Ambassador ...' – **Jacquie Turner, PS-Magazine.com**

'Jacky Newcomb, The Angel Lady – the world's leading expert on all things paranormal, shares her knowledge in an exciting, inspiring, easy style. Jacky is a warm and loving angelic envoy [who] predicted two and a half years ago that my book would be published and successful ... she was right. Let her light and inspire you as she did me.' – **Joylina Goodings, internationally renowned TV and media spiritual consultant, teacher and author of *Your Angel Journey***

'... Jacky is the UK's leading author on Angels ...' – **Spiritual ConneXtions**

'Jacky – This world is a better place because you are in it, thanks from my heart ... you are an angel.' – **Barbara Meiklejohn-Free, 'The Highland Seer' and author of *Awakening Your Inner Seer***

'Many people have paranormal experiences. Jacky Newcomb explains the phenomenon in an easy-to-understand, non-threatening way.' – **Jordan McAuley, ContactAnyCelebrity.com**

'Jacky Newcomb's extensive knowledge is generously passed to the reader like drops of liquid gold ...' – **Jenny Smedley, TV presenter and author of *Pets have Souls Too* and *Soul Angels***

'Jacky Newcomb is a warm and spectacular person ... extremely inspirational and gifted ... Her spark ignites even the most sceptical of hearts and a moment in her company makes you feel like you have been touched by someone very special.' – **Laura Wells, editor of *The Psychic Voice***

I Can See Angels

Comforting true stories
from the afterlife

By the Same Author

I Can See Angels

Comforting true stories from the afterlife

Jacky Newcomb

HAY HOUSE

Australia • Canada • Hong Kong • India
South Africa • United Kingdom • United States

First published and distributed in the United Kingdom by:
Hay House UK Ltd, 292B Kensal Rd, London W10 5BE. Tel.: (44) 20 8962 1230;
Fax: (44) 20 8962 1239. www.hayhouse.co.uk

Published and distributed in the United States of America by:
Hay House, Inc., PO Box 5100, Carlsbad, CA 92018-5100. Tel.: (1) 760 431 7695 or
(800) 654 5126; Fax: (1) 760 431 6948 or (800) 650 5115. www.hayhouse.com

Published and distributed in Australia by:
Hay House Australia Ltd, 18/36 Ralph St, Alexandria NSW 2015.
Tel.: (61) 2 9669 4299; Fax: (61) 2 9669 4144. www.hayhouse.com.au

Published and distributed in the Republic of South Africa by:
Hay House SA (Pty), Ltd, PO Box 990, Witkoppen 2068. Tel./Fax: (27) 11 467 8904.
www.hayhouse.co.za

Published and distributed in India by:
Hay House Publishers India, Muskaan Complex, Plot No.3, B-2, Vasant Kunj, New
Delhi – 110 070. Tel.: (91) 11 4176 1620; Fax: (91) 11 4176 1630. www.hayhouse.co.in

Distributed in Canada by:
Raincoast, 9050 Shaughnessy St, Vancouver, BC V6P 6E5. Tel.: (1) 604 323 7100;
Fax: (1) 604 323 2600

A catalogue record for this book is available from the British Library.
ISBN 978-1-84850-065-5

Printed and bound in Great Britain by CPI Bookmarque, Croydon CR0 4TD.

This paper is manufactured from material sourced from forests certified according to
strict environmental, social and economical standards.

I dedicate this book to you my lovely fans; to those I have met and those I have not; my friends online, on Twitter and Facebook (especially Sharon, Lilian, Karen, Rachel, Julie and Julie, as my Admin Angels and for the endless support you give me), and those of you I meet in the chat rooms ... as well as all the many people who travel to visit me at talks and book signings around the country.

I love you all. May your angels always be at your side.

'The reports of my death have been greatly exaggerated.'
– Mark Twain

There's an Angel in My Life

Angel can you help me?
I need an angel hug,
And lots of sparkly energy
And an angel's special love.
Some days can be a challenge,
And life can be so tough,
The road ahead looks difficult,
The path is very rough.
When an Angel walks beside you,
You're never all alone,
With support and protection
These gifts you'll always own.
There's an angel in my life
And an angel by my side
His signs they may be subtle
But our love you can't divide.

– Jacky Newcomb

Contents

Part 1

More of My Psychic Adventures

1

Flying with the Angels

In the beginning God created the heaven and the earth.
And the earth was without form, and void;
and darkness was upon the face of the deep.
And the Spirit of God moved upon the face of the waters.
And God said, Let there be light: and there was light.
And God saw the light, that it was good:
and God divided the light from the darkness.
And God called the light Day, and the darkness he called Night.
And the evening and the morning were the first day.
– King James Bible, Gen. 1:1-5

IN THE BEGINNING

'Why are you here? You're dead, aren't you?' I asked the young man in front of me. He smiled and walked towards the spare chair opposite where I was sitting. The chairs were the only two things in an otherwise empty room.

His name was Guy. He was an old school friend and he'd died of cancer several years previously, yet here he was, large as life and very much alive … in my dream!

3

Guy had been the boyfriend of a dear friend of mine. He was certainly no saint in life and led what you'd call a 'full life' in his short life. He was always in trouble at school, but usually for things like teasing the teachers. The class loved him, naturally, and he always had lots of friends.

I remember one time when he and another school friend got into trouble with the vicar – up to no good in the churchyard. Who knows what they'd been up to? A loveable rogue, you would call him. The vicar set them to work at the church, litter-picking in the churchyard, but it wasn't long before the vicar was handing the two boys colas and snacks … beguiled by the charm of this cheeky chappie. Guy was naughty, but not bad. My mum remembers one day Guy came round to our house and devoured a sausage sandwich she'd made him. Just normal, everyday memories.

In the years before his death he'd moved away. I hadn't seen him for a long time. Why, then, was he standing here now … in front of me?

'I'm here because I can be' was the simple reply from this spirit. 'I'm here because I've been asked to visit, to talk to you …' he trailed off.

My body was asleep in bed but my mind was wide awake. This was no dream! Rather bizarrely, we talked for a while. I knew the information was important. Then he had to leave. What had we discussed during this visit from heaven? Whatever it was, I wasn't supposed to remember.

'Wait …' I called out as he turned to leave. 'Don't you want me to pass on any messages to your relatives?' He just shook his head and smiled knowingly before walking through a door and disappearing into the light beyond.

Now I was alone in this dream room: me, two chairs and nothing else. Then I woke up. Immediately I felt excited. I'd never had an experience anything like it. It wasn't a dream, so what was it? Had Guy visited for real? Everything was clear except the full extent of our conversation. I knew important information was exchanged, but it was information for my 'spirit', not my conscious mind. Whatever Guy told me that day, I wasn't supposed to remember the details, only the experience. And remember it I did.

Over 25 years later I still remember that night, and only now do I recall the details of why he came.

My life's role was to dictate the stories of the afterlife. Others would come and visit in the still of night to share wisdom and knowledge from the afterlife. Still more would visit loved ones around the world, and I was to dictate their gifts from spirit, sharing their experiences with anyone who would listen.

Life continues after physical death, and it was time the good people knew. Life – and love – were eternal. God was our creator, our mother and our father; everything was of and from this one true source. We are all ONE.

My mission … should I choose to accept it … would take me on a wild ride, sometimes fun, sometimes sad, sometimes simply exhilarating. I would write books, articles, appear on television, meet famous people, do regular interviews on the radio and feature in newspapers and magazines. Did I want to accept my 'mission'? I accepted.

Then my mind closed off this information, where it lay dormant for many years until my body was ready to begin its journey. One day I was ready … and so it began.

While writing this last couple of paragraphs the words flowed on their own as if written by another hand. I momentarily became lost within myself, somewhere deep inside my mind ... for just a few moments, while the words scribed themselves upon the page.

I was brought back sharply to the 'here and now' by my cat jumping up and down against the window. Something had caught her attention and she wanted it, swiping wildly through the glass. Looking closer I discovered a pair of white butterflies – but outside the window, not inside with the cat! Butterflies have long been a sign of spirit contact, so I marvelled at this little coincidence. Was this a little sign from above? I hoped so.

Guy was right. Many more did come, more spirits ready to pass on their heavenly messages. First there was Uncle Eric, Dad's brother. Eric's visits were clear and vivid. We always talked for the longest time. He was a funny man and nothing had changed for him on the other side. He was funny in heaven, too! Regular readers will already be familiar with tales of Eric, and you can find some of his stories in my previous books.

Guy's personality was more mature in the 'dream-visit' ... or visitation, as I'd come to call this experience. Eric seemed more immature – full of life and lots of fun. Underneath I knew he was wise. Laughter was his teaching style.

Long-dead relatives would pop in to say hello. Usually their visits were very brief ... moments, a whisper of time.

Eric would bring other relatives to visit. He seemed to be helping them, as if buddy-sharing an oxygen tank with a fellow 'diver'. His presence meant they could hang around in the atmosphere for three seconds instead of one.

Eric was special. He had the ability to stay longer than anyone else, and although I didn't realize it at the time, this was something to do with his advanced spiritual work. Like learning a new language or working the VCR, Eric had mastered the art of visiting the earth-plane from the other side of life by appearing in dream-visits – visitations. This was part of what he did ... for a 'living' ... his job as a dead man.

I wasn't the only family member to see this loving relative. He appeared to each of my three sisters on many occasions, and even one of my brothers-in-law saw this funny man after he'd passed over.

Eric was preparing us all. Life existed after physical death and the best way forward was to visit often so that we became familiar with this phenomenon. Each time Eric called on a family member in a dream-visitation, we'd share the news with everyone in the family. Every experience was a gift for us all.

In time we learned other communication arts and practised séances at home using an 'angel board' – a safe type of Ouija board. I guessed that loved ones turned immediately into angels when they died – wings sprouting from their backs. Eric showed us that this wasn't the case. Personalities remain much intact ... at least at first. The spirits can be a little wiser, with more knowledge of life-and-death matters. They often had glimpses into our life on this side of the divide.

Eric taught us that spirits visit loved ones on the Earth for many reasons, and continue to express an interest in their relatives' lives. Weddings, birthdays and new births are of particular curiosity to the passed-over spirit. The deceased want the living to know that they are safe and well ... happy in their new dimension.

Some folk sensed the visiting spirits in the subtlest of ways, by getting a 'sense of the energy' that the deceased carry with them even after death. It's possible to 'feel' when the spirit of a loved one steps close. On occasion the air around you will suddenly become freezing cold; I've always had a tingling feeling in my body before a whispered message of love from the other side.

Over the years that followed I began 'collecting' these afterlife communication stories – aware that I needed to compile and then share these extraordinary examples of after-death communication. This was my role and, although I hadn't fully assimilated the message from so many years before, on some level I knew that this was my role on Earth.

Dad outlived his brother Eric by many, many years, but when his time finally came he joined his brother and couldn't wait to let us know he'd arrived safely in the afterlife. Hysterically funny dreams ensued in which the two of them appeared to many family members floating on clouds in swimwear, driving around in funny sports cars and generally having a good time.

His wife (Mum), daughters, grandchildren and family friends all had afterlife contact from this loving man. Dad and his brother were together again, and 12 months later ready to start their mission.

Eric began to move very much into the background as Dad stepped into the limelight. Dad was now chief spiritual advisor, and daughters and grandchildren each saw him in turn in dream visits. First he showed us how he'd died. Following one simple pain to the chest (he had had a heart attack), he'd left his body and found himself immediately on the other side of life. I was surprised he didn't go through the 'traditional' tunnel of light. Perhaps some people are aware of the journey and others are not?

When Dad passed he was greeted by other relatives who were waiting for him, heaven-side. This is a common phenomenon. Nurses and those that sit with the dying will often report how the dying have conversations with 'people' that no one else can see. Dad showed all of this to his family in a variety of dream-visits – and we began to piece together, like a jigsaw puzzle, his story of the afterlife.

Dad had himself been visited a few months before he died. He shared his extraordinary experience with me. Dad's grandfather and two aunts came to collect him when he was seriously ill in hospital. 'We're ready for you, Ron …' they encouraged, but Dad was having none of it and turned them down. 'I'm not ready yet,' he said. His own deceased family were ready to escort him to the afterlife, but he had other ideas.

I'm not sure how long you can put off the inevitable, but I know of others who've said 'no thanks' when near to death. Some of us at least have a choice on whether to live or die when the crucial moment comes.

Instead Dad found himself floating out of his body. His soul soared way above his head and left his physical body lying in the hospital bed below him. In his out-of-body condition Dad's spirit suddenly became lucid and very aware. His mind, way up on the ceiling, was working independently of his body in the hospital bed below.

Immediately Dad recalled my books and research. He was proud of his daughter and had read a couple of my books previously, and realized what was happening to him. Dad decided to come and visit me at home, and floated all the way to my house to find me! The next morning he excitedly recounted his experience to me and was disappointed that I'd not seen him when he'd visited me at home … in his 'spirit body'.

Dad lived a few more weeks after his out-of-body experience, which gave him plenty of time to say goodbye to his family, and time for us to prepare ourselves for his passing. His time was close.

Many of us have out-of-body experiences – I've had several myself, and not every spirit trip means one is near to death … not even most spirit trips mean this, but I recognized several 'signs' within Dad's experience … Dad's close encounter meant, 'It's nearly time to say goodbye …'

Once he passed over to the other side, one of my sisters, Madeline, and I began documenting the many afterlife contacts Dad made since his passing. He was determined in his efforts to show us that his life had continued. His persistence was endless and he worked hard to ensure that we knew he had made it safely to the other side of life.

Not everyone is lucky enough to have these amazing encounters, but I knew one day these stories would become a book … and so it will. (I'll let you know when we're ready to publish it!) His 'after death' was almost more extraordinary than his life, and it was still full of love as he was himself in life. Dad knew that I would write about our family afterlife contacts with him … and share them with the world … broadcast them to anyone who would listen! I'm sure that is why we had so much contact from him after his death. Dad's visits were for everyone.

He first showed us his journey as a spirit, letting us know what happened to his spirit after he had passed. Then he let us know whom he was meeting on the other side, and then next he began to just pop in and say hello. In some of his visits he was giving us glimpses of the future or letting us have little warnings, then finally his visits became more about spiritual knowledge. Dad is a great teacher on the other side.

Two weeks after Dad passed over I took part in a radio interview about life after death. I was stunned that I felt comfortable talking about his passing. The memory was still fresh … raw, but my beliefs … my knowing that Dad was safe (although in some other dimension) made it easier to talk about, to discuss the man we loved so much who'd been so recently snatched away.

Our contact experiences made the perfect examples of what happens after physical death. The radio interview was intimate. I sat in the dark at home and chatted to the presenter like he was an old friend, forgetting that I was talking to thousands of people. Real-life experiences were simpler to understand than me just 'explaining' it. People were enthralled and bemused by my stories of contact from the afterlife! I humoured myself by imagining what it would be like to listen to this bizarre conversation on the radio … this recently grieving daughter who was talking about her dad coming to visit her in dreams … a great adventure!

His adventures – and ours – are, as I've mentioned, a whole other book in themselves, but suffice to say that, over a year later, he's still visiting (although much less often). I remembered years ago asking the spirit of my late Uncle Eric to come and pluck me out of my body and take me to the other side of life … just on a trip, you understand! I was desperate to take part in their afterlife activities and wanted to know what life was like on the other side. What was it like in heaven?

Uncle Eric refused because he told me I would need to be dead to have this adventure … although I'd read about others who'd been lucky enough to go on such afterlife journeys! But this wasn't the end of this story …

I'd been going through a difficult time. My husband was out of work, I'd just had an operation and was in a lot of pain and now I was having heart palpations … and the doctors didn't know why. I was tired … and stressed, and I wanted my dad. One night I stamped my feet and howled out tears of frustration. 'Where are you, Dad? I miss you … where are you? I need you!' I thumped my fists on the pillow before rolling myself into a ball and falling into a deep sleep. I'd been abandoned … or so I thought.

At some point during the night I became lucid and aware. I was flying in the air with two people at my side. Immediately I realized who they were. Next to me was some sort of guardian angel or guide. This guide was my Dad's afterlife helper Peter, and next to him was Dad. As we flew through the air I could feel the breeze as it went past us as well as the sensations of movement. Dad and his guide were flying solo but I had some sort of 'flying machine' above my head … I felt it was there to make me feel better rather than because I needed this help. Later, as I became more confident, the flying machine disappeared.

Why were we up here? The guide began to swoop down low and I could see Dad's reassuring smile, although he didn't move any closer to me. Dad and I followed the guide and we seemed to be flying over the tops of properties.

'What are we doing?' I asked.

It was the guide who answered me. 'We're checking out suitable properties.' He replied, as we flew over the tops of some newly built, modern apartments. I realized immediately why. My eldest daughter Charlotte and her boyfriend Rob were looking for their first home together. Dad and the guide were checking things out for them. Well, well!

'We do this sort of thing a lot,' the guide continued. I nodded.

Then right away we were flying high up in the air again and carrying on with our journey. Almost immediately we came across a grey-and-black cloud. The cloud was thick and 'sticky' and I was told that this was some sort of vortex of energy – like a portal. It was hard for me to follow them and to push through, but I did it. Something was wrong on the other side, but this was the most important part of the mission. This is why they had come … this is what I was to be shown.

I had no concept of time … we could have been in the past or the future, and anywhere in the world. As we pushed through the clouds and out the other side, I saw a beach far below me – we were coming in to land. The sandy beach area was full of people and I knew we were seeing the aftermath of some sort of disaster or accident. Women were crying and some were holding babies. Dad and his guide flew down and gently extracted a couple of babies from their mothers' arms. 'What are they doing?' I wondered. Dad and Peter began explaining to the women that they were taking the babies to a place where they could continue to live. Then I realized what was happening and was totally shocked. The babies had died in this disaster. Dad and his guide were escorting the baby-spirits to the heavenly realms!

The spirits were being gently carried to heaven where they could continue to be cared for. Someone handed me a baby-spirit and I held it close. I felt great compassion for the mother of this child, a child who had lived such a short earthly life. I also felt the pain of the mother – confusion, fear, shock – but I knew that the baby was completely fine.

Only very special spirits get to do this work … I heard. Escorting babies to the afterlife is the privilege of the chosen few. 'I' wasn't a 'chosen one', but Dad was. This was Dad's work now. This was what he was doing … and I felt ashamed. I'd been moaning and feeling abandoned, crying out for my Dad, and yet Dad had a new life – one in which he had an important role.

After loved ones pass we have to LIVE – really live, learn and love. Dad had his own work and his own new life, but was still part of our life too. He was still available to visit from time to time, but I couldn't summon him up every time I had a problem! He wasn't my own personal slave … bless him! I understood the message and felt humbled.

I lifted the baby up into the air, and as I did so I noticed that Dad and his guide had two young ones each. This was a busy night and very sad, but the love which came from these special spirits brought me close to tears. These little ones were going home to God … in the arms of two amazing 'angels'.

We made one final stop along the way … we were picking up a toddler from a motorway service station … we could have been anywhere in the world … or even on another world, I wasn't sure. I was stunned at these armfuls of children crossing over – and it was then that I woke up.

I sat up in bed with tears streaming down my face. I felt distressed and helpless, but in some way accepting that it was the order of things: life, birth, death and then life again. Many years ago I'd asked if I could visit the other side with Eric, and although I was unable to do it at that time, Dad had taken me on a very privileged working trip when he came to *this side* of life. They'd done everything they could to help me and show me.

Dad never got too close to me during our trip. He'd appeared to me many times in dreams previously, and nearly every time we'd hugged – it felt so real. Two of my sisters had even danced with him on his dream-visitations – he'd been such a good ballroom dancer in life. This time he needed to make some distance between us, and I understood.

I miss you, Dad … and I always will. But I understand now. 'No more tantrums!' I vowed. It was time to get on with my job whilst he got on with his.

2

Onwards and Upwards

'If trouble hearing Angels song with thine ears,
try listening with thy heart.' – **Meriel Stelliger**

SPREADING THE ANGEL'S MESSAGE ... SOCIAL NETWORKING SITES

A lot of the past year has included looking for new ways of sharing the angel message. The social networking site Facebook was a great place to start, and I soon became addicted to chatting to fans ... and celebrities ... about angels and the afterlife on my internet page.

Twitter, the 'micro-networking site', is another great internet opportunity. You start off with one or two 'friends' or 'followers' and then, before you know it, that figure turns into hundreds and then thousands.

I love being able to keep in touch with people this way, and fans seem excited at the idea of being able to communicate with me directly. It's so easy to update the page throughout the day ... but easy to get side-tracked! I also have a Facebook 'fan page' and my wonderful 'Admin Angels' (volunteers who monitor the site and contribute) also do their own thing, occasionally giving free mini angel readings and angel workshops, right there on the site for people to enjoy.

If you want to interact with me, then Facebook is the easiest way. Visit my website and click on the link to join up … if you haven't already done so (it's easy if you have internet access). If you're addicted to angels, then this is another way to get a daily fix! Come and join us.

Fans also share their wonderful angel and afterlife experiences on Facebook, creating an endless source of inspiration for all of us.

… RADIO

As well as the usual round of radio interviews, I've also been asked to do many smaller internet 'radio' shows. I never mind if I'm talking to ten people or ten thousand; I love them all. I had to go and buy a special headphone and microphone set (mostly the internet shows are done either over the phone or via Skype connection). Keeping up with the new technology is challenging for me (but worth the effort).

The good thing about the internet shows is that many websites leave the interviews on the internet so that you can tune in to them long after the show has been 'recorded'. Those of you who are computer literate can also find a wealth of free information online.

We managed to find some old radio interviews we had on disc and uploaded them to 'YouTube' (a video-sharing website). In the future we will add more and more. The computer age is fantastic for sharing information with people all around the world, and stories are being sent to me from all four 'corners' of the Earth.

When I was asked to guest on the internet radio station 'Haunted 911', I didn't hesitate. There is nothing easier than plugging in your headphones and sitting in front of the computer at home. I did warn them that when I do these types of interview there is always a problem with the connection! I believe my angels and guides like to make their presence known, and it's amazing how many times the line crackles or cuts off completely … and I have brand new equipment, so it's not that. It happens over and over again.

The 'angel questions' included what type of car do I drive (a BMW) and who is my favourite film star (I don't think I have one!) and what is my favourite food (maybe I said curry!) ha ha! Still, I'm happy to answer personal questions. I think it's important that people get to know the 'real' me, so they feel they can trust me and the work that I do.

True to form, this particular show was late going out and cut out several times, so it sounds like my spirit friends interfered with the line as usual! Isn't that funny?

… NEW WEBSITES, AND MAGAZINES

I've also updated my website (www.AngelLady.co.uk) to include angel stories, letters, angel 'photos' and pictures of some of the wonderful fans I've met at events! It also includes a forum and a chat room; these are fantastic ways for people to share angel experiences and pass on knowledge for free.

I've also appeared in more and more magazines; this year's batch includes *Spirit & Destiny*, *Eternal Spirit*, *Soul & Spirit*, *Simply Health*, *Chat – it's fate*, *Dog Monthly* and *Your Cat* (yes, seriously!). My own 'cat and angel' interests combined seem particularly fascinating to people.

... THE LIBRARY

In these challenging economic times, don't forget to check out your local library for books. My own books are readily available from libraries around the world, too. Maybe you could ask for copies of books as birthday and Christmas gifts, or, rather sneakily, give copies of them as gifts and then ask to borrow them back!

SHARING STORIES

Another important development in the past couple of years is people's willingness to talk about their paranormal experiences. The wealth of information out there makes it a whole lot less embarrassing to share your own personal angel and afterlife encounters.

When I first started writing my books, most people were reluctant to write about their encounters ... for fear of ridicule. This doesn't happen in quite the same way these days. If you open up about a miraculous experience to a group of people at a party nowadays, you are likely to find that people will tell you they've encountered something similar, or they know someone who has, or they are simply fascinated with your tale. Those who want to make fun of you are in the minority now ... thankfully.

Share your stories – help spread the word! Be an ambassador to the angels, too.

EVENTS ... THE ANGELS SEND ME HELP FOR MY AILMENTS!

I love being invited to events, book signings and talks. In the summer I was invited to a healing festival in Somerset. The event was organized by Elaine and Ron in memory of the late healer, Bill

Harrison. Bill Harrison used to run the healing weekend in his garden (a big garden)! After his death the new festival was set up in Bill's honour. The event organizers began with no contacts and no money, yet Elaine told me she believed that Bill was helping from the other side. I wondered if I might get some help with my own ailments while I was there?

The fields were set up with giant marquees full of healers and exhibitors. Although the rain came down on and off, the sun lifted the water up off the fields quickly. The event was wonderful and I had the opportunity of running an angelic meditation on the Saturday, and giving an angel talk the following day.

When a speaker took over the marquee which had been set up for us to do book signings, we literally sold and signed copies of the books out of the boot of our car – what a laugh! And when a kindly lady told me after the talk that I made a 'glowing mum-to-be', I didn't have the heart to tell her I was just overweight! At least I was glowing, anyway.

I was delighted to finally meet the animal healer and author Elizabeth Whiter. We exchanged signed copies of our books and, once at home, Elizabeth in a later telephone call suggested I should be eating pumpkin seeds, as she believed they would be good for my health … a few each day. So I immediately went out and bought a packet.

Also at the healing festival was my dear friend, the author Jenny Smedley. Jenny invited us to her home for a meal and, after looking at the dark circles under my eyes, suggested that I might be intolerant of cow's milk. Jenny and her husband rarely eat sugar and they both have great figures! She suggested that, as well as making me feel better, this would help my body to find its own natural weight.

Jenny and Tony drink goat's milk and suggested I do the same. What a strong message. I'd asked the angels for a sign and they brought me this wonderful couple. Immediately we got home I bought two cartons of goat's milk. I was a bit nervous about trying the milk … especially as I could only get full-fat milk and we usually drink semi-skimmed. I'm ashamed to say it sat in the fridge, ignored, until it went out of date so I threw it away.

A few days later Jenny rang me about another matter and asked me about the goat's milk. I felt bad when I had to admit that I hadn't even tried it, so immediately sent my husband John out to buy some more. This time I decided to mix it into a low-calorie chocolate shake … that way if I hated the taste it would disguise it a little. I noticed that John had bought both full-fat and semi-skimmed, so I figured I would use up the full-fat first of all. Well, the first mouthful was just awful. The milk tasted so strong, but I persevered and drank down the whole glass full … I really found it disgusting.

The following day I figured I would give it another go and made both John and myself a cup of tea with the semi-skimmed goat's milk … it was delicious! I was stunned and told my husband, 'That is so much nicer than the full-fat milk you picked up …'

There was silence before he looked at me quizzically, 'What full-fat milk? I didn't buy any!'

I immediately rushed to the fridge and pulled out the carton. Here was the milk that I thought I had thrown away … a full eight days out of date – and I had drunk half a pint of the stuff! Well, I laughed and laughed! What a rude awakening. In comparison, the in-date semi-skimmed goat's milk is just fine, and I am proud to say that I rarely eat sugar now. The weight began to fall away immediately. I hope that lady doesn't ask me about my 'baby' next time I see her!

Very strangely, in that second telephone call Jenny *also* suggested I eat pumpkin seeds … and I don't need telling more than once! I really do believe that the angels send us humans with messages for us. I am lucky that many of my friends are especially tuned in to the angelic realms, so I guess their messages are even clearer than normal. Keep listening for messages from the angels passed through your own friends.

EVENTS – MEETING FANS

I had a wonderful time at the Harry Edwards Healing Sanctuary in Guildford; another event where I was made to feel most welcome. After my talk I was able to sign books and meet fans, and later my husband and I were treated to a lovely lunch in a private room.

At the event was another animal healer and author … Margrit Coats. I had interviewed Margit many years ago when I was editor of *Spiritual Lifestyles* magazine, but this was the first time we had met in person. Two animal healers in such a short time? Perhaps the angels are telling me something!

I love the healing energy of the Sanctuary, and the gardens are just beautiful … you can feel that angels gather here! If you get the opportunity of attending an event there, do go.

INTERVIEWING

I write for several different magazines and run my regular columns in *Chat – it's fate*, *Soul & Spirit* and *re:focus*, a health magazine. In my previous role of editor of two magazines I regularly interviewed celebrities. *Soul & Spirit* magazine expressed an interest in my interviewing celebrities about their spiritual and paranormal beliefs, so I decided to interview rock singer Suzi Quatro. Suzi has a fascinating spiritual life, and at the time of my interview lived in an old haunted house. She'd also had out-of-body experiences and clairvoyant episodes! She was a very gracious and interesting person to interview. I was particularly interested to learn that Suzi believes in angels!

Another interview I did was with the beautiful TV presenter Melissa Porter. Melissa is particularly well known for her appearances on such shows as *Escape to the Country*, *Put Your Money Where You House Is*, *Get a New Life* and *To Buy or Not to Buy*. Melissa also believes in angels and owns a stunning angel necklace. As well as going for lunch together she ended up coming back to my house (brave of me considering the TV shows she presents!). This delightful lady has since become a great friend

… I love my job!

CHANGES/ANGEL MESSAGE

Each year the angel message has changed slightly. I receive visions, signs … angel messages for me to pass on to people in my books and articles. Previous messages have included:

- To 'be' an angel: helping your neighbour or strangers in subtle ways
- To smile and share a blessing
- To share your angel and afterlife experiences
- To live with less – a more simple life
- To clean up the planet – one trash bag at a time
- To recycle
- To clutter-clear our homes
- To eat more healthily and exercise more
- To spend less money.

This year's message continues what we have already learned, but now we are to expand it to the next level. As well as eating more simply and healthily we are to grow more of our own foods. I've never known so many people keep chickens and grow their own vegetables ... even if it's just a pot of peppers on the windowsill or a few herbs.

I always do well with herbs, but my tomato plants and mushroom box were a disaster ... I guess you have to start somewhere! Everywhere you read about possible disasters for the near future on this little planet of ours, yet finally I feel the 'winds of change' as we are beginning to make a little difference. This is not the time to sit on our laurels and rest up. There is no time to feel smug, as we still have a long way to go, yet slowly, gently we are making a difference; the angels are helping.

Recycling has reached an all-time high in the UK; supermarkets are handing out fewer carrier bags than ever before (saving many millions of pounds across the board); everyone is using less water and composting their vegetable peelings.

We've recently picked up on the internet system called 'free-cycle' (you may have similar schemes in your part of the world). Freecycle is a means of advertising your unwanted goods (via email) for free collection from someone who 'requests' the product. The system works by people joining local internet groups (so you don't have far to travel to collect your wanted goods). Everything that is handed on for future use means there are fewer items going into landfill. It's amazing what people will collect, and we've given away potentially hundreds of pounds' worth of old things we no longer wanted.

Many of my friends are now sewing on missing buttons and mending old clothes ... like we always used to do. Last year's sweater is great with a new lacy trim, or you can turn the whole thing into a cushion! Less food waste is being created as it's suddenly OK to eat leftovers again. Many families who can no longer afford to go out now stay in and have 'family nights' playing games together. Challenging financial times around the world have also brought us closer together as families, and the angels are clapping their hands in glee.

IDEAS FOR THE FUTURE WELLBEING OF OUR PLANET … AND OUR LIVES/BANK BALANCES

Here are some of the ideas I am receiving. Some of you may remember doing these things as a child. Let's do them all over again!

1. Christmas – recycle old Christmas cards as gift tags; use … and then reuse gift bags (in our family the women pass round the same beautiful gift bags over and over again!); make your own decorations; remember teens prefer cash … and it usually works out cheaper to give (no wrapping required); make your own gifts (do what you're good at, or gift a home-made voucher for several hours of your time to cook, decorate or garden for the recipient); discuss the new 'rules' with your family in advance and you will probably find that everyone wants to do things the new way.

2. Cooking – it can be easier if it's one person's job to shop and cook. I label things in our fridge with 'keep off' stickers so that no one tucks into the 'spare veg' I have got in for tomorrow's dinner! Grow your own. Have a cupboard clear-out and remove foods you don't like or will probably never eat – swap with family and friends. Make sure that family

members don't just help themselves to expensive foodstuffs in the freezer! Work with a shopping list and plan meals in advance. Cook one meal for all the family (it's so liberating) – if they don't want it they can make their own (a sandwich, soup, etc., something simple from a single cupboard.) You'll be amazed; faced with a ready-cooked meal, you suddenly no longer have fussy eaters ... who wants toast when there is a hot dinner already prepared and on the table? Don't let the fruit on your garden trees go to waste: bottle, make into jam or chutney or swap with a neighbour who owns an allotment for any spare produce that he can send your way!

3. Household items – looking after the things you own is the easiest way of saving money. Need a new carpet, or does it just want cleaning? Can you repair that tear in the curtains? Perhaps the faded tablecloth can be dyed a new colour, or the old sheets made into a 'throw'? If you're not handy at these things, find a family member who is ... or someone who's prepared to give it a go!

4. Saving money – swap to energy-saving bulbs, turn off the tap or time your showers (put an egg timer in the bathroom – kids love it and three minutes is usually fine); unplug items at the wall (don't just switch them off). Walk, don't drive; share lifts to work where possible; shop once a week (freeze milk and bread!); use the library!

5. Create a more peaceful home – give things away, don't buy more. Cherish the things you own but use them every day ... don't save them just for best. Don't just keep grandma's old china cups in the cupboard! Pass on things you no longer use and everything else will suddenly seem to sparkle with energy. Follow that old saying and if you don't love it or it's

not useful, get rid of it (to someone in need/freecycle, etc. … or have a yard sale/boot sale and generate some cash). Diarize family night/game night or some family activity that is the most important night of the week. Make time for your family. Burn those beautiful candles someone gave you for Christmas two years ago before they get covered in dust on the windowsill. Use that 'only for best' hand cream before the scent goes off, and wear your best underwear today!

Life and living is about people, not things. Take care of your body, your family and your home. People want your time, not your money and, as Oprah would say, 'live your best life' today!

Millions of people around the world have seen, heard, felt and experienced angels in their lives. I'm going to take you on a magical journey where we will explore some of the ways these magical beings intervene in our human lives.

Let's start with Nicola's extraordinary experience.

Saved by Angels – for a Special Role

'Sitting in the queue of traffic on the M6 motorway, I anxiously drummed my fingers on the steering wheel. "This is going nowhere fast, is it, Ryan?" I sighed to my seven-year-old son, securely fastened by his seatbelt in the front seat next to me.

'Working as a spirit medium and psychic, I had a load of bookings for that evening in my shop. "I'm going to be so late," I moaned, taking the first turning off the motorway. Damn it! The road I had pulled onto was in an even worse state. All around me, cars were doing U-turns and heading back to the motorway. I decided to follow their lead.

'The road was pretty narrow. On one side there was a thick hedge, and on the other a deep ditch, so I had to make a three-point turn. I checked nothing was coming and pulled out across the road, and stuck the gearstick into reverse. But as I did so, a car appeared out of nowhere and came roaring towards us.

'People who've been in near-death experiences say time seems to slow down, and that is exactly how it felt to me. I opened my mouth in a slow scream as I realized that Ryan, on the passenger side, was directly in line with the oncoming vehicle. His little body would take the full impact of the crash!

'Immediately I released the clutch to try and move backwards, knowing it was hopeless. At the same time, the man driving the other car swung his steering wheel, desperately trying to swerve out of our way. His car hit the thick hedge opposite, bounced, and hit the front of my car. I now took the full impact.

'I gasped as the breath was knocked out of my body – but there was no pain. All I felt was relief that my side of the car had been hit and not Ryan's. Then I passed out.

'Next I began to feel my spirit float out of my body. From somewhere floating above the road, I saw my car spinning 180 degrees beneath me before it headed towards the embankment. Then my attention was pulled and immediately focused on the two angels standing in front of me. I've seen plenty of ghosts and spirits in my life, but never any angels. Both beings were beautiful, and taller than an ordinary human being.

'They seemed to be made entirely of light, and beautiful, like brightly coloured rainbows. One stood in front of me and the other by the passenger door. I felt surrounded by love and compassion – but although they did not utter a word, I knew they were there to stop my soul detaching from my body. It was not my time to die. Thankfully and most importantly, it was not my son's either.

'Instantly I was back in my body again as I heard my son scream, "Mum! Put the brakes on!" I responded automatically and slammed my foot on the brake, and yanked up the handbrake. The car came to an abrupt stop, just inches away from the deep ditch.

'I threw open my car door and leapt out, immediately running round to Ryan's door. I was concerned he might be severely injured. "Are you OK, love? Are you hurt?" I asked cautiously. "I'm fine Mum, just my neck hurts," he said.

'Then the driver from the other car appeared, white as a sheet, with blood trickling from a cut down his face. "I'm so, so sorry," he moaned.

' "Don't worry," I told him. "The accident was my fault – and I would like to thank you."

'He looked at me, confused. "For what?" he asked, looking puzzled. "You saved my son's life," I said. "If you hadn't swerved in the nick of time, you'd have crashed into him head-on instead of me."

'Then the pain hit me in an enormous wave. I clutched at my heart. "Ouch. That hurts," I muttered. I rang my husband William to tell him what had happened – but the pain got too much. My son took the mobile phone off me as I sank to the ground, and the other driver quickly called for an ambulance. Onlookers stood watching, they were motionless and in shock. The young lady who'd been driving the car behind us ran over to assist me. I could hear my son beginning to cry and asking for his dad to come and get us. It was a complete nightmare.

'The paramedics arrived swiftly, along with the police. The police officer took control of the situation and noted what had happened. As the paramedics loaded me onto a stretcher, I saw the two angels again. They smiled, surrounding me with a rainbow of colours. I felt safe, loved. I sent them a silent message: "Thanks for saving Ryan and me." A feeling of great calm washed over my body, and I remained calm even when the doctors looked over me and told me the bad news: "You've got a cracked sternum in two places, broken ribs, severe bruising where the seatbelt went, and shock." I was just relieved to be alive, and even more relieved to learn that Ryan did not have a scratch on him, just a bit of whiplash and, of course, shock.

'As the days went by, I realized that my injuries meant I'd never lead a "normal" life again. My spine had been damaged by the impact, and my heart weakened. "It'll be a long time before you can get out of bed," I was told. I was upset but not devastated. The angels had saved me for a reason.

'For the first few days I was in hospital, I saw them all the time. My room would be illuminated with a gorgeous golden glow while the rainbow of colours formed. I could not help but reflect on why the angels had saved me. Finally, it struck me that although I enjoyed the work I'd been doing, it did not "complete" me.

' "Here you go Mum," Ryan said, dumping a sketchpad and some brightly coloured pencils onto my bed. "This'll keep you busy!" Ryan knew that I drew portraits, however he never understood the reason behind my art. I was a natural medium and my family had recognized my gift since early childhood, so it was no surprise to my older relatives, when, at the age of 13, I suddenly woke up one day and began to draw portraits of what

I believed to be 'made up' faces! Thankfully, they recognized the images and realized that I was performing psychic art (or spiritual art, as I like to call it) and actually drawing the faces of passed-over loved ones whom I had never met.

'Over the years I'd created many portraits, but practically every picture, apart from my school work, had been done in black and white. Now I picked up the coloured pencils and immediately felt inspired to draw using them … inspired by my angels. When I left hospital, I painted acrylic portraits of people and animals – other times I used chalks or pastels to capture the abstract images that sprang up from my soul. Every step of the way, I felt the wonderful creative energy of my angels guiding me.

'At first, I painted the pictures for myself, but I soon realized how they could help others. I was capturing spirit life-force energy onto the canvas.

'I started to exhibit my work, through a gallery and website. Many people felt a deep soul connection to my images. Some recognized loved ones, angels and reincarnated spirits in my portraits. Continuing to work from home, I began to channel further images, plus healing drawings for my customers. My angels continued to visit me and explained through clairaudience that the set of colours I received for each person had healing qualities, which also triggered an aspect of enlightenment for the receiver.

'Each picture had its own special code of colour that connected to the recipient's core self; their gentle vibrations were realized from the person's higher soul. This sparked the seeds of healing, guidance and protection. I was content in my new role, however my angels had a further plan and I now realize I am only at the beginning of my new path.

'A full year passed quickly and my husband, son and I were about to visit my parents. We had recently moved to a refurbished Victorian townhouse, just weeks before. There were large steps leading from the pavement to the front door. Closing the door behind me, I proceeded down the steps and out of the gate. All of a sudden my ankle snapped and I spun 180 degrees before finally hitting the pavement at the very edge of the busy road and oncoming traffic. I screamed out in sheer pain and begged William to phone for an ambulance as I tried to sit up away from the dangerous road. My walking stick lay shattered in two pieces next to me. Panicking, William telephoned for an ambulance and then rang my parents.

'A nurse appeared from across the road, as she'd seen me fall and had come to my aid. Introducing herself as Mrs Haze, she knew my husband and wanted to make sure we had telephoned for help. Looking at her in my dazed state I saw a golden glow of colour surrounding her body, obviously it was her aura. "I saw you spinning the way you did, you completed a full half circle, I hope you have not dislocated your ankle?" Mrs Haze asked me. The pain was unbearable; the paramedics soon arrived though and rushed me to hospital with William following swiftly behind. My parents also arrived and collected my son. My leg was x-rayed and then the doctors told me the bad news: "You have an abnormal break." The doctor paused. "You've broken your leg and dislocated your ankle, we're sure you'll need an operation, and need to have a metal plate inserted." I was very concerned because I'd never really healed from the car accident. How would my body now cope with the trauma of this? Later that night, as I lay in my hospital bed, I decided to ask my angels for further guidance and prayed to them to be kept safe. I hoped they were listening …

'The following morning the anaesthetist visited me and I relayed my fears: putting on a lot of weight and having more problems with my heart. Considering all alternatives he decided not to put me fully under, but to sedate me in another way. Later that afternoon I was prepped for surgery. 'Count down from ten please, Nicola,' asked the doctor. '10, 9, 8, 7...' I was asleep …

'Becoming conscious I noted how I was surrounded by nothingness, but I could still see clearly, and more vividly than when in my normal wakeful state. I noted the doctor working on my leg; I could see my blood pumping through my body and blockages forming at the back of my calf. The nursing staff and other professionals stood below me. I could see everywhere within the room without actually moving.

Within a tenth of a second I was lying back down facing a magnificent light above me. It was tangible, I could feel it swarm around me and I could hear a harmonic sound, like the buzzing from a hive filled with bees. But I wasn't frightened. I intuitively knew that it was not a passage leading to my death.

'Muffled voices rang out louder and louder; it made me feel like I was standing on a stage in a theatre with the spotlight directly on me. The first thing I recognized was my two glorious angels, who had saved me once before. I remember silently asking them what was happening and realizing that I was having another out-of-body experience, when suddenly the light disappeared and space took its place. Many beings which I could never possibly have imagined appeared in front of me; then within seconds they were gone. I saw long tunnels, like corridors, and other areas that I can only name portals.

'There were streaks of light, which resembled lightning, although I could see orbs of light passing through them. I saw a being appear in between stars and then fade back into the darkness, like he was simply walking in space.

'My sight turned and I saw lots of areas, which resembled the Milky Way. Intuitively I knew they were other galaxies and individual universes positioned between dimensions, like high-rise flats stacked on top of each other and in many alterative directions. I was taken out past the "big bang", past the outer edge of space and into an area where everything was motionless, tranquil and at rest. I saw seven white planets, which I recognized right away: they were the seven heavens. But as quick as the visions came they went again and I suddenly found myself back in my body and fully waking up. The only problem being that I was still undergoing surgery.

'I yelled out for help, informing the doctors that I was conscious, and sadly asking them to "get my dad", as he would know what to do! I found this very amusing afterwards – the fact that I reverted back to being a child needing the reassurance of her father, despite being a married woman and a mother.

'I heard a panicked voice saying, "Just relax, Nicola, we have everything under control." That is all I remember, then I was back into a deep sleep.

'Eventually the operation was over. I responded to the sound of the anaesthetist apologizing profusely. Opening my eyes I assured him I was all right and kindly thanked him for his help. I did not feel any upset towards him, as he had listened to my concerns and sedated me appropriately, considering my health.

'I believe my angels used my sedated state of consciousness to communicate detailed images to me. I felt that I could not blame anybody for the experience. It transpired after the operation that I did indeed have a deep vein thrombosis in my calf, which is a blood clot from a blockage of blood in the veins. This was confirmation to me that my experience was real and not just an aspect of my vivid imagination.

'From that moment on, I found myself inspired to channel the energy of the beings I met within the out-of-body experience. I began to receive many messages of hope and transformation relating to the fifth and sixth dimensions and beyond, via automatic writing. My spiritual path was opening further and I have come to realize that the spirit art was just the beginning of an even more inspiring path of enlightenment.'
– www.sharnajamescreations.co.uk

Nicola's experience is breathtaking in its power. I wonder, as more and more people have out-of-body experiences and near-death experiences due to the advances of medical science ... will more of us have a glimpse into the other realms?

Shortly after reading Nicola's story I had an operation myself. I was excited to think that I might have a similar experience ... but I didn't. As I lay in the recovery room I couldn't help feeling disappointed. The last thing I remembered was the surgeon saying, 'Count backwards from ten, Mrs Newcomb, and then you'll begin to feel a little drowsy ...' And now I was awake again and the nurse was shaking me.

'Mrs Newcomb ... Jacky, are you awake?'

'Yes' (damn it!).

Part 2

Your Real-life Experiences

3

Once Upon a Dream ...

'Reality is merely an illusion, although a very persistent one.'
– Albert Einstein

Millions of people around the world see and experience angels in their lives. I'm not just talking about a wishful-thinking concept here, but real-life experiences and angelic encounters.

Often these visits occur when we're in trouble both physically and emotionally. Sometimes people see or experience angels when they are in altered states of consciousness, like Nicola in the previous chapter (unconscious or perhaps while meditating). And sometimes angels visit in dreams.

WHAT IS AN ANGEL?

An angel is an energy sent from God (or the creator) whose role is to care for and watch over their charges ... in this case, humankind, us. One of their primary roles is guardianship of the human race. They have been created to look after us. They soothe and comfort us and, in extreme cases, can even keep us out of danger. Angel experiences are mainly subtle but sometimes their signs are dramatic, to say the least … I'm going to share some of these stories later so that you can make up your own mind.

> *Angel of God, my Guardian dear,*
> *to whom His love commits me here,*
> *over this day be at my side,*
> *to light and guard, to rule and guide…*
> *Amen*
> **(Traditional Prayer)**

YOUR GUARDIAN ANGEL

The ancient Greeks believed we each had a guardian angel looking after us. Jesus taught us about angels – specifically relating to children being guarded and protected. In Genesis (in the Holy Bible) they deliver Lot from danger, and in the New Testament an angel delivers St Peter from prison.

Guardian angels form part of many belief systems including those of the Babylonians and other ancient cultures. In fact there is an angel statue (now in the British Museum) which once decorated an Assyrian palace!

Angels are just as relevant today and form part of our modern-day culture. Contemporary representations include images and words representing the angels' protection and guardian role, which appear on everything from caps to teddy bears! Angels are literally everywhere.

WHY ARE THEY HERE?

Angels long to reassure us, and they do this in many ways. They bring us gifts of a delicate touch (you might feel an angel holding your hand, or become aware of an angel placing a reassuring hand upon your shoulder, even though your physical eyes can't see a thing). Your angels may bring a massive sign; for example you might shout or cry out for help and an angel appear before you. These more dramatic experiences are usually accompanied by feelings of great peace and love, which is just as well … I imagine if you weren't frightened before the experience you could well become terrified if an angel manifested before you! During these angel interventions people report feeling calm and relaxed, almost as if they are transported to another dimension (which maybe they are).

Your angel wants to help you to fulfil your divine life purpose … to fulfil your destiny, whatever that might be. Your angel loves you unconditionally and, as I say in my guided meditations, 'Your angel knows everything about you and loves you exactly as you are … right now.'

SIGNS THEY ARE AROUND US
People long for signs that their angels are around them, and the angels are happy to oblige. Watch out for repeated words … in the newspapers, on TV or radio or in the books you are currently reading. Anything which makes your ears 'prick up' and take notice … listen! Is this a sign? Have you asked for a particular type of message and then the radio keeps playing songs with the answer to your query? Have you been worrying about something and then notice a TV programme has recorded over your pre-planned series … yet the alternative show has everything you need to answer your question?

ANGELS ON A BICYCLE?
It's important you ask your angels to take part in your life. You can take them to work or school and invite them on holiday! Imagine

them sitting in the passenger seat of your car or hitching a ride on the back of your bike. 'See' them in your mind's eye and know they are with you everywhere you go.

Sometimes their help appears in the form of a human soul; it's like the angels' alert ... and inspires our closest friends to telephone us 'out of the blue'. My friend Wendy will sometimes turn up at my door and announce 'Did you want me?' as if she'd been summoned by some unseen force. Usually I do want her ... or need a friendly ear at that exact moment. Wendy is well-tuned in to the angelic realms, like many of my close friends. Are you?

Have you ever felt an urgent need to ring an old friend or to turn up unexpectedly at their door? Perhaps you too are being summoned by the angels.

You could try this experiment. If you suddenly have a strong vision of a friend, especially if you haven't heard from them in a while, why not give them a ring? Maybe you too would be brave enough to ask them, 'Did you want me?' I'd love to hear how this worked out for you!

COMFORTING HUGS

Have you ever had an angel hug? People from all around the world write to tell me about this phenomenon. It often happens during times of extreme stress. A quiet and calmness seems to occur and unexpectedly you feel as if you are no longer alone.

People who've experienced the phenomenon say it's like they are enfolded by angel wings. Imagine being surrounded by total unconditional love. A deep inner contentment is felt by those in need. An angel has been to call and left you feeling more able to cope with the problem at hand. Ask your angels for a hug today ...

Ask for this phenomenon to occur to you if you need help.

Sometimes requesting the experience prompts them to move closer; knowing that you have given permission. Invite the angels into your life at every opportunity. Say, 'Angels, I need a hug.' Then go about your business! Wait and see what happens.

Your 'angel hug' might not be physical but might appear in the form of a special treat: a session in a hot tub, a glass of your favourite wine or the gift of a wonderful feel-good book to snuggle up with … why not treat yourself to an angel hug? … because you're worth it! If you don't need one right now, how about giving an 'angel hug' to a friend?

ANGELS IN DREAMS

Angels love to visit us in dreams, too. This isn't all 'made-up nonsense' by the sleeping mind. No! Not at all. An angel dream is unlike any other dream you've ever had. The angel dream leaves you with an actual message, or sometimes guidance. More likely they just bring love. The dreams are clear and don't fade afterwards. They stay with you for the rest of your life.

Angels can leave you with a single word or simple phrase left clearly in your mind. Sometimes you wake with a clear knowing of what to do next. Angels might come as escorts, bringing lost loved ones or pets from the other side of life … but they never tell you what to do. At all times, the choice is ours. We are the ones who decide what to do and how to do it. Angels bring reassurance, and light … a wonderful burst of healing energy for you to enjoy.

PERSONAL SAFETY

Don't ever feel tempted to test your angels by doing something crazy. Jumping off a bridge is not a good way of testing if angels are real. They can't override our free will, and if we choose to do something silly we have to suffer the consequences – it's a universal law!

Ask the angels to empower you and give you the strength to solve your own problems. The angels will love this and, ultimately, so will you. Imagine how satisfied you will be when you can turn round and say triumphantly, 'YES! I did it!' Your angels will always be at your side ... remember to ask them for a sign if you need extra reassurance.

On occasion angels will try and impress a message or warning onto you. Feeling nervous about walking alone down a dark passageway late at night? Then don't do it! Does the car feel unsafe tonight? Get it checked out immediately. Have a strong gut instinct not to go on a date with that man you don't know too well? Then don't go! Gut instinct (that feeling of dread which hits the pit of your stomach) is your angel's warning sign! Safety first at all times.

Likewise, many feel the angel's good news as a fluttering of excitement, 'butterflies' in the stomach to show when something is good and right. Learn to listen to your inner angel.

LETTING US KNOW THEY ARE OK

We long for proof that our loved ones are safe and well; that they 'made it' to the other side. This is a theme that runs through all my books and I like to share the miracle stories as new ones come in.

In some of Dad's dream-visitations he did extraordinary things, like he would appear to limp, carrying the walking stick he needed in life ... then pretend to be frail or fall before leaping up in the air, bounding up steps and generally skipping about. He likes to use these visual images to show how he was ill and frail and is now well and bounding with energy and health.

This story reminded me of those familiar dreams.

Better in Heaven

'My Dad had asthma and was diagnosed with COPD (Chronic Obstructive Pulmonary Disease), even though he never ever smoked. In June 2008, aged 72, he went into hospital with a chest infection and picked up an antibiotic-resistant bug in his lungs. We nearly lost him but he pulled through, although the hospital sent him home giving him two weeks to live and told us to say our goodbyes.

'It was a very emotional time but we never gave up hope, and my stepmum nursed him, giving him the medication from the hospital, and he seemed to be doing really well. During this time he said he was thinking about dying all the time, and you could see that it did worry him. His quality of life was never what it used to be but he was still with us and we loved him dearly.

'By Christmas his breathing started to get slightly worse, which he put down to the weather, but as the weather changed it didn't seem to make much difference, he was still very breathless. On his 73rd birthday in February we gave him his presents but he didn't even have the energy to pull the cards out of their envelopes. His breathing got much worse, and it was so upsetting to see him suffering.

'A couple of weeks later he got so bad that we had to get the doctor, and Dad was taken into hospital on Monday, 9th March. Unfortunately on the Wednesday night he had a fall and hit his head, and on Thursday morning we were called into hospital as he had taken a turn for the worse. We went in to see him and he said he'd had enough. He said he wasn't afraid but he wanted to go. Although this was so sad for us, it was a comfort to know he wasn't afraid, and I don't know what made him feel like that but something did. He passed away peacefully with his family around him at 4.30 that afternoon.

'A few days after the funeral, I remember when I went to bed that night I said to my husband that it had been the first day I hadn't cried. At about 3 a.m. that morning I woke and could smell a really strong smell … like burning, but really strong. I woke my husband, who said he couldn't smell anything. I checked around the house but couldn't find anything wrong, so I went back to bed.

'I then had what I now know is called a dream-visitation. I was having a dream but then it changed. In the new dream I was carrying my dad. He had his blue pyjamas on, which he always wore in hospital, but the day he died he'd been wearing a hospital gown because after hitting his head his pyjamas had blood on them and the nurses changed him. I went to put him down and as I looked at him his eye opened slightly. He then moved, and in my dream I said to my husband, "Look he's moving." He opened both eyes wide and gave me a lovely smile. I said "Dad, you're OK …" He said "Don't worry, I'm OK, and I don't need that" as he picked up his blue asthma inhaler and threw it as hard as he could.

'I then woke up but felt absolutely wonderful. I felt like a weight had been lifted and felt so happy that Dad was OK. I'd been looking at your book a few weeks before Dad had gone into hospital but hadn't started reading it properly yet, but did see something in there about dreams. After the dream I got your book out and re-looked at it and couldn't believe what I read. I'm so certain my experience was a real visit from Dad, and I would like to thank you for writing about this because if I hadn't read your book I would have dismissed it as just a nice dream.'

– Deb, England

KEEPING US UPDATED FROM THE OTHER SIDE OF LIFE

One thing that sceptics want is proof that the afterlife is real. Most afterlife contact is personal and intimate – loving messages rather than outright proof.

I've written before about how my late Uncle Eric came to warn me that Dad would be in danger if he had an operation here on Earth. At the time of the dream Dad wasn't due an operation, and only fell ill later that day. At the time we were on holiday abroad, so we flew Dad home and he had a simple procedure in a local hospital instead of the exploratory surgery the foreign hospital wanted to do – along with all the complications of language differences.

I believed at the time, and I have believed ever since, that my late uncle appeared in the dream to give me information that I didn't know about in advance … information that saved Dad's life. These types of dreams are rare (there have been a dozen or so of this type of experience in my books), but here is one where the deceased gives information that the receiver doesn't know about in advance … nothing mind-blowing, but enough to give that little bit of proof that people look for. I'll let Gail share her story in her own words.

Inside the Coffin

'On 3rd December 1995, my dad suddenly died without warning. Well, a few nights after his death I had what I thought was the strangest dream. I was sitting on some stairs and my surroundings were just white in colour. I was talking to my dad and, unbeknownst to me, I was actually talking out loud and my husband was listening to me, for what he said was the whole conversation. He told me I was chatting for several hours. I don't remember the whole conversation, but what I do remember freaked some members of my family a bit, even my ex-mother-in-law.

'Just before the funeral my two children, who were 9 months and 5 years old at the time, drew some drawings to put in with my father. My nephews and nieces had done the same thing, and they placed these items in envelopes, along with a photo of myself and my three sisters and my mother. These all went into my father's coffin. I had no idea what my nieces and nephews had put in their envelopes until my father told me in my dream!

'The one that sticks in my mind was my niece had put in her savings … all of 29p in hers, with a note saying, 'for your wings'. Well, as you can imagine I was shocked, and my sister was even more shocked when she asked her daughter what she'd put in her envelope. It was exactly what Dad had told me in the dream.

'Also in the dream was my ex-mother-in-law's mum, who had died before I met my ex. I told her what I'd seen and described her perfectly, even to the way she sat. Well, it made my ex-mother-in-law cry, so we knew it was for real.'

– Gail, Wales

This story gave me goosebumps when I read it. It's not an easy thing to fake, is it? … And anyway, why would you want to? When my own friend came to visit me all those years ago, the visitation was very simple. Since I've been writing up other people's experiences over the years, they seem to have got more and more complicated and clever … perhaps the energies have changed, or maybe as humankind has become more enlightened to these types of encounters so our loved ones have been able to create more meaningful messages and encounters for us? Fascinating!

WARNINGS

Usually our loved ones' messages are positive and uplifting, but sometimes their visits are to warn us about bad news. Occasionally we can change the outcome because the spiritual advice helps us make a different choice, but sometimes the dream-visits are just to give us a little glimpse into the future. I worry that these experiences aren't always helpful. It's hard enough to live in the here and now; knowing what's happening next may make us frightened …

I was given a warning dream about Dad … I was shown his possible 'life-timeline' (an indication of when he was likely to die). As he was elderly and had been ill for many, many years, this was not scary to me. This next story probably was a little bit …

The Warning

'My name is Sinead and I would just like to share my story with you. I had a dream one night that my grandmother, whom I loved as a mother and lived with all my life, came to me. She had been dead for 10 years. I'd often dreamed of her but this time was completely different. She was a small woman, but in the dream she was tall and wearing what I can only describe as a snow-white wedding dress. The white light around her was blinding me and I did notice that her feet were not touching the ground. When I was small she had this brown leather sofa which pulled out into a bed. We kids used to sleep on it.

'In the dream I was lying on this sofa and I could see my sister from the back of her head, and I touched her and she was dead. I was so upset. I asked my grandmother why and she just shook her head. I woke up and got such a fright I rang my sister and asked her if she was OK, and then told her what had happened in my dream.

My sister picked up on the white dress part and said, 'Sinead, you must be going to get married.' I have two sisters, one of whom was sick with a drug addiction, but it never crossed my mind that the dream could be about her because she'd been ill for such a long period of time.

'Within a year I was married and my sister never made it to my wedding … but it was my other sister … the one who'd been ill, not the one I rang. She died in April 2008 and I got married in the October of the same year.

'I know now that my grandmother was sending a message to tell me that when I got married my sister Deirdre wouldn't be there. I know that my grandmother had come to collect her.'
– Sinead, Ireland

HELPING TO MAKE DECISIONS

Imagine angels as your very closest friends. Your friends know you so well. They can see all sides of the problem and advise you on what they might do in the same situation. But ultimately we are born with that most basic of human abilities – that is, to choose our own life path. 'Free will' is a gift from God. We are the only ones that ultimately decide our future … for better or for worse, we learn by our own mistakes. However, kindly father that God is to us, we don't have to make our choices entirely alone! Know that your angels are always by your side, helping you.

DREAM PREMONITIONS

Dreams are amazing. Our brains love to sort and filter information. They show us suggestions, play with ideas and let us do the crazy things we wouldn't normally do during waking consciousness. But that's not all …

When your physical body is asleep, your soul is awake … and aware and having many exciting experiences all of its own. Sometimes you remember these and other times you don't.

Soul travel (also called astral travel or out-of-body experiences) can be one of these – ever dreamt that you've been flying? Felt the breeze as you move through the air like I did, or had real encounters with loved ones on the other side of life? Have you ever been visited by angels and spiritual guides? It's all real!

Many famous people have experienced dream premonitions. The 16th President of the United States, Abraham Lincoln, had a dream premonition that he was going to be assassinated. Just days before his death he was shown a vision of himself at the White House. All around him people were mourning and when, in the dream, he asked a soldier who had died, the soldier told him it was the president himself. Lincoln was killed just ten days later – it was the first assassination of a US President. Was this a sign from the 'other side' or was the President tapping into some sort of higher awareness or 'remembrance' of a pre-planned event? (see my book *Angels Watching Over Me* for more stories like this one).

According to the *Guinness Book of Records*, singer/songwriter Paul McCartney has a song which has had more cover versions recorded than any other song in history. The ex-Beatle woke from a dream one day with what he called 'a lovely tune playing in my head'. The song was 'Yesterday'!

Mary Shelley's novel *Frankenstein* was inspired by a dream, and writer Stephen King also credits dreams for the inspiration for his own scary books! Otto Loewi, the German physiologist, dreamed important information relating to the theory of the chemical transmission of the nerve impulses … which led ultimately to winning the Nobel Prize! Luckily my own dreams aren't that complicated, although I've certainly had lots of information for my books and even had the title of a book suggested to me when I was asleep!

Madame C. J. Walker started out as a woman who, in her own words, was '... from the cotton fields of the [American] South ... [and] promoted to the washtub ...' Madame Walker was suffering from a scalp condition when she had her dream, and used the ingredients she had been shown to create a very successful haircare product which helped to reverse the condition and loss of hair. She went on to become a millionaire after founding her own company to manufacture and sell the product!

Elias Howe invented the sewing machine after a 'spear dream' gave him the idea of adding a hole to the end of the needle, and golf professional Jack Nicklaus was shown how to correct his golf 'swing' in a dream! What's going on here?

When we sleep our minds do a whole lot more than random dreaming. When we sleep our minds are free to wander ... sometimes they seem able to tap into this universal library of information, and of course, at other times, our deceased loved ones use this 'dream state' to come and visit us.

THE BOOK OF LIFE

The book of life is a 'place' on the astral realms (the finer-density heavenly realms) which is said to record every thought, deed and action of the whole of humankind. The records are sometimes called the Akashic Records or Hall of Records, and have existed since the beginning of time. *Akasha* is a Sanskrit word which translates to 'space' or 'ether'.

Many ancient cultures believed in the existence of these records, and many psychics, including the seer Nostradamus (1503–66) and Edgar Cayce (1877–1945, also called the sleeping prophet), 'plugged into' these records. After the tragedy of 9/11, more people searched online for the Nostradamus prophecies than for any news station.

As well as details of our earlier and past lives, the records are also said to house our possible future (or most likely future) outcomes. It's probable that prophetic dreams (those where we discover the future) happen when we accidentally stray into these 'records'.

If we fall asleep following a very relaxing day, it's possible to accidentally encounter these Akashic records (or library realms/ dream state) and read the 'future' and even the past. Some psychics seem to have the natural ability to do this. They tap into these records while in a relaxed state … maybe occasionally we all do this?

DREAM TRAVEL … OR OUT-OF-BODY EXPERIENCES

Many, many people have had what we call 'out-of-body' experiences. They literally feel their soul-body lift out of their physical body to fly free and independent. Sounds crazy? Not at all. It happens most often during illnesses and accidents, but some people have these experiences on a regular basis … for no apparent reason at all. 'Flying dreams' can feel very real. You can feel the air as it blows past you and you can visit places you have never been before … even flying through sold brick walls.

Your perspective might be the same as if you were flying in a helicopter. People often see things from the 'air' that it's not possible to see from the ground, and there are many recorded cases where their 'OBE' visions have proven to be correct in the physical sense. What they saw out of their body actually exists in real life!

When your soul flies free from your body it can connect to many different dimensions and other realms … be open to exciting possibilities in your 'astral-life'!

Many people (both adults and children) have experienced out-of-body travel, which can range from simply floating above the physical body during sleep to visiting other countries or realms.

Sally had an out-of-body experience when she was giving birth.

A Higher Place of Safety

'My son was born prematurely at 34 weeks old and I was very frightened that he would be handicapped in some way. He was my firstborn and I had visions of a baby with no legs or arms, as he was too early and not "finished off".

'It's a stupid thought when you think about things rationally. The birth was very long as he was not ready to be born, and I was exhausted. He was too far down the birth canal to have a caesarean so we had to just carry on. The birth had began at 8 a.m. and it was now 3 a.m. and I was past caring what happened to me and just wanted it all to be over.

'The baby was in difficulty and people seemed to rush in from everywhere to save him. I don't really know what happened then or how I got there, but the next thing I remember was being on the ceiling looking down at my body and all the people trying to help me. It was not for long and I was not frightened. Then I was back and my son was born. He spent two weeks in an incubator but he is now a 6-foot tall 13-year-old boy, in perfect health and very bright.

'I have always thought that maybe I nearly died during childbirth, but after reading one of your books I have changed my mind. I now wonder if I had an out-of-body experience because I was so tired and distressed. I always felt like I was able to take time out to recharge my batteries. Perhaps someone was helping me?'
– **Sally, Wales**

The multi-talented rock singer and radio presenter Suzi Quatro once told me that she uses astral travel to visit her friends, and will then report back to them what they were doing at the time she visited in her astral 'body!' Now that sounds like fun!

Sometimes people write and tell me about spirits who come to collect them or communicate with them – to escort them on their dream travels. Remember when I was flying with Dad, he was accompanied by his own guide Peter? Terri had this experience happen over and over again:

'I was in the middle of a dream when it seemed to get interrupted; I heard the noise of wind above my head and then felt a strong pushing sensation over my right shoulder, followed by a female voice in my right ear saying, "Communicate with me!" She said this three times.

'A few days later I was lying in bed with my eyes shut. I was awake but I thought that someone or something was in my room walking around. I thought it was my daughter but it wasn't. I heard the wind noise again but this time it was quieter. Then I felt as though someone was leaning over me on my right. I heard a different female voice whispering in my right ear, saying, "You'll be fine, follow me."

'Many other experiences followed, not all positive, and the voices continued; after my first two experiences I went and bought a video camera with night vision, and have since recorded lots of orbs on camera. One night I recorded my remote control being "pushed" or "thrown" from a windowsill, and on three separate occasions caught my cigarettes and lighter being "pushed" or "thrown".'

It seems like some spirits are desperate to let themselves be seen to be believed!

NEAR-DEATH EXPERIENCES

Many feel they leave their body during a near-death experience (NDE), which often happens when the body is in crisis. You don't have to die when you have this experience … and it's not, as some people believe, a 'dream' at all.

Upwards of 15 million people are thought to have experienced leaving the body during a near-death experience, finding themselves separated from and floating above the body. Sometimes 'other realms' or planets are seen, and certainly people have witnessed angels, guides and deceased relatives, as well as deceased pets! This can be similar to the dream-visitation experience where loved ones on the other side of life visit in dreams.

Actor Gary Busey says he actually saw the 'grim reaper' (the angel of death) after he had a motorbike accident back in December 1988.

Here's a real-life experience sent to me by a reader.

Ignored Dream Warning

'When I was 16 I had a terrible time. I was living in Bury with my parents, had just left school with no qualifications and was living on a large council estate surrounded by crime. I really felt as if I had no future.

'I felt cut off from the mainstream of society and I guess you could call me "a rebel without a cause". The only way I knew how to live my life was the system of "survival of the fittest".

'One night during a disturbed sleep I had a nightmare. I was full of fear as I got into the passenger seat of a car, but in the rush I failed to fasten my seatbelt. The next thing I remember was speeding off in the car. We turned a bend in the road and crashed into a stationary car which was parked on the wrong side of the road.

'Everything went black and then I woke up in bed in a sweat. I was really shocked but at the same time relieved that it was only a dream … I could have died!

'Then a week later I found myself getting into the same car … for real. My mate seemed in a hurry and said it was because he was being followed, so I opened the car door and jumped in. My mate shouted at me to shut the door fast.

'All of a sudden I got a feeling of déjà vu … this reminded me of my dream, and a feeling of dread came over me. I felt as though I was stood next to myself outside the car, as if I was a spirit and was just about to get in, and felt powerless knowing what was going to happen next. I fought hard and felt myself go back "into" my body instantly, and then I tried to get in the back, knowing I couldn't control my body long, but the back door was locked! The whole experience was bizarre.

'It was another vision but this time I was awake. Then I heard my mate shout at me to get in … just as I had "seen" in the dream. My mate was insistent so I stupidly got in. At least I remembered the seatbelt from the dream, but when I went to fasten it I realized it was broken! This was a nightmare for real now …

'My friend wasn't an experienced driver and quickly lost control of the car. He yelled out, "I've lost it" as we were turning a corner. Then I felt us hit something and heard a loud crash before everything went black.

'I drifted in darkness for a long time until I caught sight of a light up ahead of me. I felt drawn to this light because it was warm and inviting in the pitch-black darkness.

'When I got nearer I saw it was perfectly round. Three figures stood in front of the light but I couldn't make out their features. Their silhouettes looked black against this brilliant yellow golden light. In my head I wondered, "Where am I? Why am I here?" Then a reply came back to me from these figures, who told me, "Your time isn't up yet … go back." I was slammed back into my body and woke up on the pavement bleeding from cuts all over my face from the windscreen.

'I found out later that my mate had stolen the car. I had a major operation and spent 16 weeks in Burchill Eye Hospital recovering. When they took off the bandages I was blind in my left eye, but luckily I could see out of my right eye.

'When I was released I went back home but I felt changed somehow, especially after thinking of my dream and the accident. I had been warned in my dream and the split-second visions, but I didn't listen. Even so it was clear that someone had been with me the whole time. I felt reborn, but reborn without fear, without hate and without negative vibrations inside my head! I was a new man then and I became aware of my own spirituality, something I'd never thought about before. I was completely "at one" with myself.

'Strange things began to happen then and in the following years I became aware that I could hear or feel things that others could not. The experience certainly changed the path of my life and I became more spiritual as a result.'

– Ian, England

4

Reassurance

'If ever there is tomorrow when we're not together, there is something you must always remember – you are braver than you believe, stronger than you seem, and smarter than you think. But the most important thing is, even if we're apart I'll always be with you.'
– Christopher Robin to Winnie the Pooh

Don't we all just need a little love and reassurance from time to time? Isn't it nice to know that someone is always by your side; that our loved ones are always keeping an eye on things from the other side of life? After losing her grandmother, this lady was devastated … but luckily her grandmother showed that things are not always what they seem. Rachel wrote to share this delightful story.

See You at the Wedding

'In December 2007 my beautiful grandmother passed away. She was a wonderful woman and was loved very much. I was getting married six months later and really wanted her to be there; I just couldn't believe she was gone, and wanted to call the whole lot off, I was so upset.

'Then a couple of weeks later I had this amazing dream. In the dream I knocked on my grandmother's door and my aunty, who lived with her, let me in. My aunty wouldn't let me into the living room at first, she wanted to explain to me that there was someone waiting to see me.

'When I walked into the room my grandmother was sitting there! I couldn't believe it and I started to cry hysterically because I knew she had died. I immediately went back out and sat on the stairs, sobbing. Then my uncle came over to me and he told me to calm down and not to be afraid because my grandmother had come back to see us ... because we wouldn't let her go. He told me to relax and let her talk to me.

'I calmed down a little and my grandmother came out onto the stairs and sat beside me. She put her arm around me and told me not to worry. She said she was sorry she couldn't make my wedding in person (in the physical sense) but that she'd still be there in spirit. She said she was looking forward to the day and would be so proud of me. She said that when I took my first dance as a married woman she'd be beside me dancing with my grandfather. I was stunned but couldn't believe it. I was sobbing so hard so she just hugged me then and said goodbye.

'When I woke up I felt great ... and relieved somehow. I couldn't get the dream out of my head for days and could remember every single bit of it when normally I can never recall my dreams. This was nothing like a normal dream at all.

'It was a brilliant experience and in the end my grandparents did come to the wedding. In the photograph that someone took

of me and my new husband having our first dance together, there's the biggest orb of light right beside me!'
– Rachel, Ireland

Isn't this story just delightful? Don't you love knowing that your relatives on the other side can still make the wedding?! I think it just goes to show that sometimes those orbs of light on photographs (which people call dust, light flares, flash glare, etc.) can have other meanings entirely!

One lady from America sent me a totally enchanting photograph taken at her wedding; although a whole series of photographs were taken, just one showed 20 or so 'orbs' of light … shaped like angels!

If you're interested, I do have a page of 'angel photographs' that readers have sent me at my website: go and check them out for yourself at www.AngelLady.co.uk.

This next story is just wonderful, too.

Angel Helps a Nurse

'I feel very lucky because I have experienced many signs and reassurances from my angels. I often see white feathers which float down so gently, always when I need them most. I feel that I am open to the many ways that the angels choose to communicate with me, and have used these experiences to convert many sceptical friends and family.

'My mum, who is also very spiritual, bought my sister and me a perpetual calendar which contained a different thought about angels for each day. During this time I was a student nurse and this involved placements on many different hospital wards. During a particular placement I was assigned a mentor who would be responsible for me while on that ward. The ward was extremely busy and was a very daunting experience as a novice! From the offset I felt totally unsupported by my mentor. I kept telling myself that she was a very busy nurse and that things would improve, but I constantly felt in her way and that I was a just a nuisance to her.

'I feel that I am quite a strong person and I'm able to think positively about most situations, but as the weeks progressed and things didn't improve, I began to really doubt my abilities as a nurse and dreaded going in to work.

'During one particular shift my mentor had barely spoken to me and even during break would never try to make conversation. I left that night feeling so down, and cried most of the way home. When I arrived home I was certain I was not going back to the ward and was feeling so inadequate. However a phone-call from my mum helped me to see things more clearly, and I did go to work the following morning.

'I can't begin to tell you how different this shift was. From walking onto the ward it felt different, like a light had come on. My mentor greeted me so nicely that I was taken aback, and she explained that she had arranged for me to follow a patient to theatre and stay for the operation. I left that day feeling so different to the night before, like I was starting to find my role within the team.

'When I arrived home, the first thing I did was call my mum. During the conversation she asked what my calendar had said that morning. I realized I had run out of the house without turning it over, something I normally do religiously each morning. The verses are so uplifting, but I had never had one so specific. It had both my mum and me in tears. I felt that I was meant to read it then, as it would not have meant half as much to me if I'd read it before work. It said: "A surgeon's hand, a friend's note, and a mentor's pat on the back are all angels in the guise of the ordinary – carrying us like a thousand lifting wings."

'I could not ask for a clearer sign that I have an angel providing me with constant protection and love. It's a lovely feeling to have when you feel low at points in your life.

'PS I received the "friend's note" part of the message later that evening when a friend sent me a text saying she hoped I was enjoying my placement!'
– Lucy, Wales

As humans we do have to make the final choices and decisions about our life ourselves, but that doesn't mean we have to do anything alone. Angels can give us the strength to carry on or to make the big and scary changes that are sometimes necessary. Changes can be very positive, but fear can often mean that we do nothing at all … thereby automatically 'failing' at our task, which is a real shame.

Remember to ask your angels to give you the courage to make the changes you need to make in your life. Here is a story of bravery … all done with a little help from our feathered friends from above.

Angels of Protection
'My first "real" angel encounter was in 1997. I'd divorced a wonderful husband in 1974 to pursue my career in show business. It was an amicable parting. Sadly he died in 1989 and I always regretted following my career, because he was a good man.

'Then in 1993, at the tail-end of my career, I met the man I thought I would be spending the rest of my life with. In the beginning he was all I could have hoped for in a husband, but he soon became abusive and manipulative. I suffered five years of absolute hell at his hands. The whole thing had been a very big mistake and my body was covered in bruises from his beatings.

'Then in 1997, while I was alone in my house … following another physical attack, I found myself in great despair and called out to Heaven for someone to help me. Almost immediately I was aware of "someone" else there with me, and a sort of calm and peace descended upon me. Then I saw a vision of a most beautiful angel telling me that all would be well. He told me that he was there to protect me and that I was safe. It felt like a huge warm duvet being wrapped around me, and I knew at that moment I was going to be all right.

'That experience gave me the power to change things and to get my abuser out of my life. Three months after that I had successfully "ejected" him from my home. Two years later I sold my house and moved 102 miles away to a lovely little house by the sea near my daughter and grandchildren, and I've been happy ever since.

'Shortly after I moved to Southsea I bought my first set of angel cards, and while I was looking through them I gasped at the picture of Archangel Michael. It was "my" angel, and when I read about him I knew I was right: strong and protective. So he has been my "Guardian Angel" for the past 12 years.

'My one box of angel cards has now increased to six boxes and I consult the cards daily.'

– Pat, England

Now I'd like to share this beautiful angel story from Australia … it helps to reinforce the message that our loved ones are around for the important occasions in our lives.

Necklace from Australia

'I was five years old when I went to Australia with my mother and father to visit my grandparents on my father's side. I remember it very clearly, especially meeting my grandmother and grandfather. I even remember the room I stayed in because it was so lovely and I have lots of memories from the whole holiday.

'My father also had a sister who lived in Australia and I have a clear recollection of my visit to her house and meeting her two daughters, my cousins. When I arrived back home to England my aunt sent me a necklace. It was made in the shape of a map of Australia, and I clearly recall sitting down to write a thank-you note. The whole trip was a very important part of my childhood.

'Sadly, years later my mum and dad split up. I was 10 at the time and my father went to live with another woman. My aunt in Australia still continued to send Christmas cards to us and kept in touch all through the years. I was grateful to know that my mum sent Christmas cards back to them with little letters on how the family were keeping.

'As my father got older he became ill with emphysema and for many years he didn't write to his sister in Australia. I felt really sad that he didn't keep in touch because I knew my aunt asked about him often.

'I decided to try and keep in touch myself and I wrote to my aunt one Christmas time, and about five years ago I enclosed a picture of me; I was 25 by that time and I told her I still had the necklace she'd sent me (although I had no idea where it was). I tried searching for it and couldn't find it, but I knew it was somewhere in my room.

'One evening about three weeks later I was sitting in the bath and I was thinking about Australia, and wondering if my letter had arrived and if I would get a reply. I also thought about my childhood memories of my grandmother and grandfather.

I went to step out of the bath and my body became freezing cold, and I had the urge to get back in the bath, which I did. After about five minutes I stepped out of the bath again and grabbed my towel – and as I looked down my necklace was on the bathroom mat! I was completely stunned! How had it suddenly appeared from nowhere after being missing for so many years?

'I yelled to my mum and asked her if she had been wearing it or found it; she replied no and asked why. I told her I had just found it on the bathroom mat and I think she was as surprised as I was. I tried to think of an alternative explanation, like maybe one of my nieces or nephews had found it and dropped it, but even so I believe "somebody" … maybe an angel … brought my necklace back to me that day.'

– Lynne, England

Some of these stories do give me the shivers! Many people say that they feel a cold chill when a spirit is present. Maybe this was the cold that Lynne felt when her necklace was being brought to her? By the way, just for reference … a spiritual appearance of an object is called an 'apport' (the disappearance of an object by spiritual means is called an 'asport').

Nicola wrote to share her daughter's experience with me. Children find it so much easier than adults to just accept what happens without needing explanations!

Operation Angel

'My daughter Natallie broke her arm and unfortunately had to go to theatre to get her arm reset. When she woke up she told me that she'd had a dream about a beautiful angel. I was so happy that she wasn't alone during this experience – it actually made me cry.

'Natallie is 10 and unfortunately she can't remember anything else apart from the fact that the angel was female and that she was sitting with her during the operation (and when she was unconscious).

'I reassured her it must have been her guardian angel looking after her and, strangely, once the anaesthetic had worn off she couldn't even remember telling me about it!'

– Nicola, England

Because children have so many of these types of experiences I've devoted a whole chapter to it later in the book.

SAYING GOODBYE

Common to the visitation experience is deceased loved ones coming to say goodbye to their living relatives in the hours and days before they pass. When someone crosses over after a long illness, they may be 'fluid' in the body for some while beforehand.

The husband of a friend of mine was dying of cancer. He used to fly free from his body every single day, and regularly communicated with his deceased mother as well as 'fly' around the neighbourhood to old childhood haunts (in his 'out-of-body' state) in the weeks before he physically passed over.

Dads say goodbye to sons, aunts to nieces, grandads to grandchildren, and so on. It shows that sometimes even though the body is physically alive, the spirit may well have already partly moved on to its new heavenly home. This can be especially comforting when the 'body' appears to be suffering … all is not what it seems.

A deceased uncle came to me in a dream once. His god-daughter had been involved in a serious accident and was in a coma. He told me that her spirit was with him on the other side of life already. Strangely, although this young woman didn't pass over physically for nearly two more years, she never regained consciousness. My uncle was right!

Always Here for You

'Mum and I always spoke about what would happen if either of us passed over and we both had the firm belief that there was life after death. We realized that whoever went first would be given the chance to prove it to the other.

'Mum was a devoted Christian who went to church every week and had 100 per cent faith, but she also had an understanding of a life after life and a knowing that here or there we would be able to communicate in one way or another. She always joked, "You'll never know where I am or when I'm watching …"

'It was a Sunday morning and I was sleeping over at my sister's house. My husband was out of the country and I often stay with her at weekends because we are so close. My four-year-old daughter was in bed with me and it was about 7.45

a.m. She had stirred, which woke me, but I quickly settled back to sleep. At this point I had a very vivid dream where my mum was talking to me about passing. She was talking to me as though she had already passed on, but was reassuring me with her words, saying, "You know I'm not gone … I am always near and if you want to talk to me you can, and you know I will listen."

'I woke with the conversation on my mind and the feeling as though Mum had already died. I quickly dismissed the feelings and went about my day, and then 15 minutes later I was in the living room with my sister when the phone rang. It was Dad and he said he was struggling to wake Mum, she was breathing but only just. My sister told him to call an ambulance and we jumped in the car to drive over to my Mum and Dad's. On the way I told my sister about the dream and I found myself getting upset because I knew Mum had already gone.

'When we pulled up outside the house the ambulance had already arrived. It rushed Mum off to the hospital. Sadly, 15 minutes later the doctors came and told us the bad news. She'd had a massive stroke and wouldn't recover. They told us she would probably last 24–48 hours. They told us they would make Mum comfortable and there was nothing more they could do.

'Mum did pass 48 hours later, just as the doctors had warned us. It was very peaceful. When I worked it out later I realized that when Mum came to me in the dream she'd already had her stroke, and although Mum was physically here on this side of life I believe her spirit had already passed over.

'It gave me great comfort to know that Mum was able to say goodbye, reminding me that she's only a thought away and also giving me that knowledge and conformation that there is life after death. She still helps me through today ... she is my angel on my shoulder!'

– Sharon, England

FOLLOWING THE REGULAR ROUTINE

It's not uncommon for spirits to appear in a familiar way after they pass. The grandma who always telephoned you on Sunday evenings will wake you up in the night with the sound of the phone ringing, for example. Others dream of chatting to deceased loved ones on 'the phone'.

If your late brother's favourite outfit was a black t-shirt and jeans, the chances are that he will appear in a dream-visit to you dressed the same way. Sometimes we are simply relaxing ... barely what you would class as 'asleep' at all ... their visit can completely catch us off-guard and for just the briefest moment, we forget completely that they have died at all ...

Here Again in Cyprus

'My father and stepmother retired to Cyprus shortly before my father's passing (late in 2004) from cancer. He was well known in Cyprus because he'd had property there and spent many long years visiting the area.

'This was my first visit since his death and walking down the 'Main Street' in old town Famagusta took me nearly two hours because everyone wanted to pass on condolences; such was the effect he had on people. Dad was very well loved and it was a nice feeling.

'Later that week I was sitting round by the pool at my step-mother's house. The children were in the water and my wife was discussing something with our friends and my stepmother (whom I'm very close to). It was a lovely warm day and I'd just started to doze off.

'There was a small bakery next door that we used a lot. My father would go in there and buy pastries and sweets for us all to have for lunch. He would suddenly appear next to the pool carrying the bag of food proudly, and my stepmother always told him off for spoiling the kids and eating too much … and getting fat! I know this was only in jest, as she really loved him!

'I'm not sure now if I was asleep or nearly asleep, but I heard footsteps and looked up. There was my dad with a bag of food coming to join us. I smiled and sat up in readiness, I think I even waved. Then I came back to reality … what was I thinking of? My dad wasn't coming to join us because he'd passed on.

'I was so sure it was him and that it had really happened. I was quite shocked for a while afterwards. No one else saw anything at all, and my wife said I had only been dreaming and the children were unaware, too. I was shocked, and shed a tear, but I was also so sure it was true that I just felt sort of relaxed, as this was a "normal happening", and no doubt we would have shared a cheese pastry together.

'Was he really there? Was I dreaming because of where I was and the emotion? Or, as I now believe, was he trying to make things appear normal by bringing the food to me in the vision?

'To add to my shock, last night, not only was I possibly "joined" by someone, not only was I now believing I did see my father, but I could smell pastries and bread cooking! This smell lured me out of my room and downstairs, and there was my wife baking biscotti, a favourite of my dad's. Why was she baking at 11 o'clock at night, and why biscotti? She said she "just fancied it" at that time. Perhaps, after all, it was my father's hand again.'
– James, England

GETTING THE MESSAGE THROUGH

The loss of a loved one can be such a burden to carry. We long to know by any means that they are still around us, still care for us, and generally to make sure that they are safe and well.

The challenge from the other side of life is to try and reach out to us across time and space to ensure a message is received and, more importantly, that it has been understood.

This delicate procedure can cause misunderstandings ... and sometimes reaching out can create more problems than it solves.

Case History 1
The Message from the Other Side

A grandfather manages to appear in his granddaughter's dream. He indicates that he has come from a shiny bright tunnel of light and asks her if she wants to accompany him ... one day.

The Misunderstanding

This young woman has three small children of her own. She is now terrified that Grandad's message means she will be dying, too.

Grandad is trying to indicate in a clumsy way that time is different on his side of life and that, although for us the time of our parting seems immense and often lonely, from his perspective life and death are separated by no time at all.

Grandad's reassurance is completely misunderstood and his granddaughter has to be persuaded that she has nothing to worry about – Grandad isn't coming to collect her for many years!

Case History 2
The Message from the Other Side

Desperate to reassure his son that he has made it safely to heaven, Jim tries night after night to reach out to his son Alex in a dream.

Due to his grieving pattern, Alex often lies awake for hours at night and then falls into such a deep sleep that his deceased father cannot reach out to him in any way.

One night Jim decides to visit Alex's best friend Marty instead. Marty remembers Jim but is not suffering from the grief that son Alex is, so Jim is able to pass on a message that he is OK and has made it safely to heaven. He is keen to let his son know that he no longer feels any pain.

The Misunderstanding

The following morning Marty shares his 'strange dream' with his mate Alex, but rather than being excited at the message Alex feels bitter and resentful. If his Dad loved him, why didn't he visit him in his own dream? Why on Earth would Dad pass on a message though Marty, a person he hardly knew?

Of course we can immediately see that Dad did everything in his power to get a message to his loving son, and must have felt devastated that the hard work had not been appreciated! It's possible that he might have decided not to try again for fear of causing more harm.

These misunderstandings occur on a regular basis – although this is certainly not the intention of our loved ones heaven-side.

Dream-visitations have occurred for many years but with the birth of the internet are now more widely reported. My books are full of loving contact stories from the other side. Regular readers will now know that these afterlife communication stories are for everyone in the family to enjoy and benefit from. Our deceased loved ones reach out to whomever they can get to – this might be a child or even a neighbour. Acknowledge the loving symbolism behind the visit and know that your loved one crossed the ocean of different dimensions to accomplish this task as a special gift for you and your family.

Sometimes I receive troubled emails from people who have received dream-visits from loved ones that they simply don't understand:

- A loved one tries to speak to them and they can't hear what is said (the loved one is trying out a visit for the first time and is not experienced at delivery – they just want to say 'Hi I am here and I love you').
- A loved one reaches out and you try to touch them … immediately they disappear (it takes a lot of work to appear in this form and it can be impossible to see them and touch them at the same time in the dream). They are not disappearing on purpose or as a way of frightening you.
- You beg for years for a loved one to appear to you in a dream, and when they finally make it, all you see is their face materialize for a couple of seconds before fading away. (Appearing in our dimension is like holding your breath under water – they are doing their best, so be grateful for any contact you receive!).

Here is a letter from Theresa in Ireland which explains this point entirely.

'I lost my dad when I was 12. I was not prepared for his death and still miss him deeply 15 years on. My mum has eight children and two are younger than me. I always wanted Dad to appear to me but this never happened. However, my sister, who is three

years younger than me, was lucky enough to get a visit from him several months after he died. She was sitting in my brother's bedroom when he appeared and she was able to have a short conversation with him.
'I admit I am a little jealous but I am glad to know he is OK and can come back.'

Theresa does understand the challenges, and even though she didn't receive the message personally she is aware enough to know that the dream-visitations are for everyone to share.

CONCLUSION

Life continues after the physical body dies. This life consists of the continuation of the existence of the soul and the personality. The soul (complete with personality) moves to a new dimension – the one which we call heaven. The soul does not suddenly become an angel but does have a wider perspective on life and death (depending on how advanced the soul is). Sometimes they can see a little ahead in our own life and can come back to give us advice (even though they probably aren't supposed to do so!).

Souls like to keep in contact with their loved ones on Earth, but for many reasons which we don't fully understand, this is very difficult. They also like to keep an eye on events on Earth (new babies, weddings, etc.).

Many souls are now aware that it's possible to come back to this side of life (some say God gives them permission to do so), to say goodbye one last time. Not every soul is expert at this procedure, but they do the very best they can.

This visit might involve appearing in a dream or affecting objects around you. They can flicker lights, set off alarm clocks and smoke alarms, or simply draw your attention to a song on the radio (there are many more stories on this phenomenon in my previous books on the subject).

The existence of life after life is real and there are literally millions of examples of real-life contact stories which prove this.

Now let's look at some more great stories!

5

It's a Miracle

'Miracles are not contrary to nature, but only contrary to what we know about nature.' – Saint Augustine

Miracles are experiences which fall outside of the laws of nature … or perhaps that should be 'outside of the explainable laws of nature'. Often associated with religion or God, miracles are experiences where divine intervention changes a life … or more likely saves a life. Miracles are wondrous happenings with no logical or 'normal' explanation – but of course this might well work as an explanation for many of the stories in this book!

I love to read about your stories of mysterious strangers who arrive just in time to help save your life and then disappear inexplicably. I love a good mystery!

Here is Angela's story.

Sink or Swim

'In the summer of 2006 I was living in Spain. My daughter and I and a few friends went to the beach one day after school for a picnic. The sea was quite rough as there had been a storm a few days before. Being cautious, we told the girls they could only paddle in the shallows and not go in any further.

'As we were eating, a middle-aged couple went for a swim right in front of us. Suddenly a young man appeared running towards the life-ring, he grabbed it and ran into the sea. We couldn't understand whom he was trying to save, as the couple were the only people in the sea and they weren't shouting or waving. As he entered the water he threw the rope at the middle-aged woman to hold but she didn't see it, so I went to help.

'As the man was getting further into the sea so was the rope, so I went in too. The water was only below my knees when suddenly there was nothing under my feet! I fell into a channel and was hit by a very strong force which immediately took me out to sea. I was approximately 200 metres out and fighting for my life …

'I tried so hard to swim back in to shore but I wasn't getting anywhere, I couldn't make it past the waves. Then the water started to drag me under and I couldn't help but swallow great mouthfuls. I was drowning!

'I lost all my energy so quickly, and then it hit me … I wasn't going to get back to shore. I had nothing left in me to fight and I started to go down. I wasn't scared but I was angry. I immediately accepted that I was going to die but knew that I still had so much to do in my life; the worst thing was that my little daughter was stood with my friends watching this all happen. She was going to see her mother die …

'As I took what I thought was my last breath, something caught my eye. It was the orange life ring. The young man had saved the middle-aged woman's life, taken her to shore and then my friend had told him I was now in trouble, too. This very brave young man came back out into the treacherous water to save me, too.

'Somehow I found the strength to push myself up. He tied my hands onto the ring and told me I'd be fine. Then he towed me back to shore. His eyes never left mine the whole time.

'I don't know how this man ever had the energy to save two lives in that rough water that day, but he did. He took me back to the beach, tied the life ring up again and then walked off.

'I never had the chance to thank him for what he had given me, so I tried to find him by contacting the local papers and radio but I never heard from him again. I truly believe he was an angel; something I never believed in before.

'I had nightmares for a long time after that, and it changed my life for ever. It took me a long time to realize that my experience that day was the start of my new life. We none of us realize when our lives can be taken away.

'I became interested in Reiki healing and I met a lady who worked with angels too. She gave me a reading and said that an angel had done something to me that had changed my life forever … 18 months ago. How did she know? This was the time of my "accident".

'From then on I was hooked! How did she know this about me? Had the angels told her?

'She told me that angels will help me if I just ask them, so I started talking to them. My life has changed so much since I found the angels in my life. I have always been a very positive person but now I know anything is possible if you just ask. I am so excited about my new life and now want to help others in some way.'

– Angela, Spain/England

I too had a near-drowning incident, but my experience happened when I was just a young girl. Just at the point where I felt I was going to die, I felt a presence come to help me. I never saw my saviour, as Angela did, but it changed my life for ever too. Sometimes you don't know what you've got 'til it's gone (as the song goes), or in my case 'nearly gone'; maybe it's time to start living your 'new life' today? Why wait until you nearly die to live the life of your dreams … the life you want for yourself? It's something to think about.

Saved from the Bulldozer

'I was a typical 15-year-old and have a vivid memory of a day I snuck into a deserted building with some cider. It seemed the perfect hiding place at the time and I was happy thinking that I was alone and safe.

'I hadn't been sat there for very long when suddenly I had this overwhelming feeling that I had to get out of the building. I can only describe it as urgent, and it grew so intense and "desperate" that I threw the bottle down and scarpered outside, leaving my precious drink behind!

'This place was a local haunt for teenagers to smoke and drink so was often full of kids. When I got outside, the building was surrounded by workmen with a bulldozer ready to knock the building down. I was completely stunned. No one had mentioned this place was being demolished. I'd obviously snuck in when they were having their lunch-break.

'I'll never forget the shocked look on one of the builder's faces just before they were ready to bulldoze the building. He gasped, "My God there's a kid in there!"

'I'm now 40 and I have never forgotten that moment to this day. Who warned me, because I know that information didn't

come from any normal source? I know for a fact that an angel was looking out for me that day and it saved my life.'
– Teresa, England

These feelings of urgency to move, stop or even stay are what some people call 'gut instinct'. Others call it natural intuition, but of course I believe that it's our guardian angels keeping us out of trouble. Listen carefully for your inner voice ... it might just be trying to save your life!

Angel on a Plane

'In April 2007, my partner Mark and I were on our way back from a great holiday in Spain. We boarded the plane as normal and all was well for a short time, when suddenly the passenger behind my partner started swearing, shouting and grabbing the back of my partner's chair, and generally making us all feel very uncomfortable. This woman was hysterical, and was scaring us all to death.

'Mark was looking very pale and concerned, and I was trying, with difficulty, to focus on my magazine. By coincidence I noticed the article in the magazine was all about guardian angels, so I turned to Mark and started to talk to him about the feature with the intention of relaxing him a little. I took the opportunity of praying to the angels for our safe return. I asked for a white feather as a sign ... although I hadn't really considered that this might prove a little difficult being so high up in the sky!

'Luckily we arrived back safely and I never told anybody I had asked for help ... or a feather sign. Then a couple of weeks later I went to the spiritualist church. I was delighted to be chosen for a psychic reading and was stunned when the reader asked me if I'd asked angels for help? She told me they were spiritually handing me a white feather.

'The story brought a tear to my eye because I hadn't told a soul about my request. Clearly "someone" had heard me.

'I do believe our loved ones come back from the other side, too. My cousin and grandma visit me often and alert me to their presence. My house alarm and smoke detectors go off for no reason, lights flicker and candles have flown across the room on several occasions!

'My dog barks and wags his tail … at the wall! On several occasions I've asked the dog, "Who is it? Who can you see?" Then one week when I visited the church again the reader told me to stop saying "Who is it?" because, she said, "It's your gran!"

'It makes me feel all warm inside to know my family are still around me. These days I just say "Hi" when I feel them with me.'
– Ann-Marie, England

Here's another story of angels looking out for us.

Angels Watching Over a Sleeping Child?
'My name is Kaz and I have an eight-year-old daughter. I would never normally do anything like this, but I got your book *An Angel Held my Hand* for my birthday and I haven't stopped reading it all day. Reading a couple of the stories has made me realize how many times my own angels have intervened in my life.

'One night I was going to bed and had the urge to just check in on my daughter, Taylor. I had just bought a small night-light which we put on the floor next to her bed, as the cord wouldn't reach to the bedside table. Taylor must have got hot during the evening and pushed her quilt off. I noticed it was half hanging off the edge of the bed and was now lying on top of the lamp. I was shocked to discover that the bulb in the lamp had already melted through the plastic, burnt through the quilt cover and was now burning into the quilt itself.

'If I hadn't checked on Taylor I'm sure the quilt would have caught alight. An angel intervention was the first thing I thought of. My daughter has spoken several times about "ghosts" she has seen and spoken to … perhaps they are angels, too!'
– Karen, England

Have you ever wondered if the faerie realms are real? This next story is unusual but it's by no means the only story I've heard like this. When I was researching my faerie book, *A Faerie Treasury* (co-authored with Alicen Geddes-Ward and also published by Hay House), we came across loads and loads of real-life faerie encounters (although I'll admit, not as many stories as I find about angels).

Philip Solomon is a respected medium and radio presenter … he has nothing to gain by sharing this experience with me. Don't they say that truth is stranger than fiction?! Here is Philip's experience exactly as he sent it to me in an email (reprinted with permission).

Goblin Surprise

'Jacky, did you ever read my autobiography, *Guided by the Light*? To tell you the truth, I never used to believe in fairies, but there's a story in there you might find interesting.

'When I was a young man working for the Decca Recording Company, I was walking across the fields to the old factory one day, in the company of a junior record producer and friend, when we both saw quite clearly what you could only describe as a tiny green man (like a goblin), walk right across our path in front of us. He looked up and smiled, skipped down the hill and vanished!

'My friend always used to ask my wife in later years, "How did Philip work that trick?" But it was no trick Jacky, we really did see a goblin, fairy, whatever you want to call it that day!'
– Philip Solomon, England

Miracle … or magic? Life isn't always what it seems! For the record, a psychic once told me that I would one day move into a house with a woodland at the back. There I would encounter a faerie … I'll keep you posted!

If this story has caught your interest, go and search out a copy of our book, which includes many real-life faerie encounters.

Crossing Guards

'My story took place a long time ago. I was just 15 years old at the time and was shopping in Kent. I needed to cross the road and waited at the zebra crossing for the lights to change. This took "forever" but eventually the lights turned green and the car nearest me stopped.

'Knowing it was now safe to cross I stepped onto the zebra crossing, but was immediately pulled back onto the pavement by someone grabbing the back of my jacket. Before I even had time to react, a car came speeding round the bend and drove into the back of the car nearest me, pushing it over the zebra crossing … right where I should have been standing. It was so close it brushed my clothes as it skidded past me.

'Shocked at witnessing the accident and realizing what a close call I'd had, I spun round to thank the person behind me for their help. They'd saved me from injury and maybe even death. I would surely have been lying in the road under the front car if this person hadn't pulled me out of its path. Yet when I turned round, no one was there.

'I knew it was an angel instinctively, and thanked him or her immediately. That day is as clear today as it was then. I was in the wrong place at the wrong time … it clearly wasn't "my time" to go. That is one day I will never forget.'
– Debbie, England

These magical miracles occur all over the world. So many people have been touched by an angel in some way or another. It's wonderful to feel we are cared for and loved in the unconditional way that only an angel can love us. These experiences bring great joy and peace into our lives and, best of all, those who experience an angel in their lives never forget what happened to them.

Angel encounters of all kinds are etched onto the memory for life and passed down from generation to generation for all to share. Isn't it wonderful to be able to read angel stories in books, too? I never tire of reading angel stories myself.

Let's look at another mystical miracle.

Dad's Special Protection
'I lived with my partner Harry for seven years. The first year was fine, but after that things went rapidly downhill. He was a lovely man and would do anything for anyone when he was

sober, but when he'd had a few pints he was horrible. He was violent towards me and it wouldn't be too over the top to say he became evil!

'He would fall in the door, drunk, but always managed to get up to punch and kick me around. This happened, I would say, five out of seven nights every week. This went on for six years before I found the courage and strength to leave. I have my dad to thank for giving me that courage and strength.

'My dad had died four years earlier and he never believed in the afterlife, as my mum, my sisters and I all did, but he came to me anyway. It was one night after I had been beaten worse than any other time. I was lying in bed next to my partner at about 3 a.m., too afraid to sleep in case he roused up and started hitting me again, which he often did.

'My deceased dad appeared in the bedroom and came and sat on my side of the bed and said, "Hello, love." I whispered to him to speak quietly so that he wouldn't wake Harry up. My dad promised me that Harry would not wake up while we were talking. He sat stroking my swollen and bruised face, my black eyes and split lips, and the pain eased considerably while we talked. He went on to tell me that many times, when my partner had been strangling me, I had been sent back here because it wasn't my time to go. He said that the time had come when I really must leave Harry before he did me any permanent damage, and that my two babies had been protected by the angels each time I was pregnant and being used as a "punch-bag" and "football" by my abusive husband.

'Dad said that he would help me to get a house and keep myself and my babies safe while we got away from my partner. My eldest was 11-and-a-half months old and I was one week away from the due date of my second baby's birth. I gave Dad my word that we would leave the next time my partner went to the pub, because then I knew that I would have a few hours to get our things out. My dad then told me that he would have to go now and I must go to sleep and rest because my partner would not be waking up again that night and I would be safe. I slept then without fear for the first time in many years.

'For once I was glad when my partner went to the pub the next day; I knew he wouldn't be home until after midnight. I got together all of the baby things, cot, pram and double buggy, ready for my next baby. I gathered up all of our clothes and we went back to my mum. I had only been there a day when I went into labour in the evening and had my second daughter at 3.27 the next morning.

'After leaving hospital two days later I put my name down on a housing association list, and three months later my two daughters and I moved into our new home. We hadn't got much to start with but I gradually built up my belongings and furniture and we were happy at last.

'It's 29 years since I left Harry, and although I had a couple of boyfriends when I was younger, and even another daughter, I could never trust any man enough to actually live with one again so I have raised my daughters by myself. I've decided to live the rest of my life alone. At least that way I know that no man will ever harm me again. I have my dad to thank for coming to see me and getting me out of a dangerous relationship. I have never seen my dad again, but I know he is looking after us and always will … thank you, Dad.'

– Kathleen, England

Kathleen's story is very special indeed because her dad was able to give her lifesaving advice from the other side. How many of us would find the courage to leave in the same situation? With her late father by her side … her very own guardian angel, Kathleen knew she would be safe. What a blessing!

If this situation is familiar to you, then do know that you have your own guardian angels who are there waiting to help you. Get help from human friends, too, and make your plan so you can get away safely when the time presents itself. You deserve only the very best, and never forget it.

Fire!

'Twenty-eight years ago I was young and foolish. Some days I dabbled with Ouija boards. I would gather friends for an evening of contacting those who had passed. This particular evening I had called on my mother as our guide, as always. Towards the end of the messages she gave a message that we all believed was for my friend. She spelled out, "Fat Fire, Will Burn Right Arm, Do Not Worry, I Shall Look After The Children." It was a scary message and we were a bit frightened by it, to be honest.

'Some months passed and it was nearing Christmas, and I had been invited out for the evening. On returning home at almost 2 in the morning, I headed straight for the kitchen for a glass of milk and switched on the light. No light? So I guessed that the bulb must have blown.

'When I went upstairs I noticed the small lamp in my bedroom was on and my partner said, "No, there is nothing wrong with the kitchen light; we had a fire in there and it is black with soot!" It was my custom to cook a huge Indian curry for the weekend and I always made my own papadums, which had to be cooked in a shallow frying pan.

'Apparently my partner decided to have second helpings late that evening. He put on the chip pan to melt the oil for the fry pan and then decided to go upstairs to the toilet, completely forgetting about the chip pan. While he was taking his time in the toilet someone knocked on the front door. Thinking it was me, and angry at the late hour, he ignored it. Then someone knocked a second time, much louder, and he shouted, "You will have to wait!" The third knock completely shook the house! Opening the toilet door in anger, it hit him that the house was full of smoke, black and acrid.

'"Oh my God, the chip pan!" He ran down the stairs into the kitchen and everything was ablaze: the blinds, the ceiling lightshade melting and dripping onto the floor tiles, igniting them also. His first reaction was to pick up the chip pan with a wet tea towel and place it on the floor while dowsing the flames elsewhere. He opened the front door and the air hit the flaming pan and it ignited again. He threw it out the door, setting fire to the hedge! What a nightmare. Then he rushed back into the house for the children. He ran into their bedrooms, opened their windows and made sure they were breathing. He went back downstairs and the door was still open. He looked at the unbroken snow by the front door and wondered … "Who had knocked on the door?"

'His arm was hurt and he had an angry burn along his *right* arm. It was some weeks before my friend said to me, "That was supposed to happen to me!" I had not made the connection at all; but I believe my mum was there at my door, to look after her grandchildren. Who else could have been knocking on my door without leaving footprints along my long pathway?'
– Ava, England

Ava's experience is another one of those stories that gives you the shivers. How can you explain this strange story? A neighbour who might have noticed the fire would surely have stayed to help, not disappeared into the night. You just know that something other-worldly is going on here.

House fires can happen in an instant. I've gone to bed on more than one occasion and left candles alight in the downstairs rooms … by accident, of course. On other occasions I've put on pans of food and walked out of the room and completely forgotten about them until I've heard the smoke alarm yelling out its warning.

Make sure you have smoke alarms in your house and that they are working. It's also a good idea to use a kitchen timer when cooking food and never, ever walk out of a room when you are cooking with fat!

Thank goodness Ava's family were all safe … with her mum's help from the other side of life.

This next miracle story comes from Manitoba in Canada.

Tractor Angel Saved My Life

'I have believed in angels for quite a long time, and when I received gift cards from my daughters for my birthday in November and for Christmas, I waited until I got the inspiration to buy some books. Shortly after Boxing Day I went to a bookstore in our local mall and purchased four books: three novels and one of your angel books. I'd planned on buying a fourth novel but I heard a voice in my head tell me to put it down and search for a book about true angel happenings. I didn't have any idea where to look for books on true angel experiences, and although there were many people in the store, there wasn't anyone near me. The next thing I recall was hearing a voice behind me asking me what I was looking for. The girl had on a employee shirt of the store I was in and directed me immediately to the section I wanted, which wasn't far from where I was standing. I saw your books on the shelf and felt immediately drawn to them, so I picked one up to purchase. When I turned around to thank the girl, she wasn't anywhere to be found!

'While reading the stories in the book, it brought to mind things that have happened to me in my own life, where I feel that angels have helped me.

'I was a big truck construction driver at one time and I drove materials used for constructing roads, parking lots and other hauling. I had to spread crushed limestone that was used in the rural areas to make their roads. The box that holds the material is in an elevated position, and my job is to move in a slow, forward motion spreading the limestone. My checker would let me know when the box was empty, with a hand signal telling me I was in a safe position to let the box down. Normal procedure is to get out of the tractor and make sure there isn't any leftover debris on the tyres or back of the box before I drive on the roads.

'As I was getting out of the tractor one time I heard a voice loudly telling me to "Get back in." I immediately sat back in my tractor and crouched in my seat to look in my side-view mirrors so I could see the back of my trailer. The box wasn't coming down; then I started to see sparks. I looked out of the rear window of the day cab of my tractor and saw my box had got caught up in hydro power lines, which was extremely dangerous and potentially life-threatening. Electricity was now going through my entire tractor and sparks were flying everywhere.

The tyres on my dump trailer caught fire, and if I hadn't listened to that voice I would have died.

'We managed to sort the fire out quickly and everything was OK, but I had a near miss that day.

'After reading most of your book, I came across a part where you explained that we need to ask our guardian angels for help, and I knew I would always remember those words. I have since changed professions and now work in car sales. One day recently I somehow managed to drop my glasses in about a foot of snow and couldn't find them anywhere. I was working with a customer so decided I would have a look for them after he had gone. As soon as I finished the sale, I remembered the part in your book about asking angels for help, so I figured I would ask if I could get my glasses back … it certainly wouldn't hurt, anyway.

'As I was signing our time book to end my day, our receptionist told me that someone had come to her counter and dropped of a pair of glasses! I asked who'd brought them up and she said she didn't know the person. They just brought them in and left. Maybe it was an angel – who knows? But at least I got them back.'

– Noel, Canada

Yes, the glasses could have been coincidence, but where did the warning voice on the tractor come from? Interesting …

This events in this next story started off in a normal way … then things just went from bad to worse.

Launderette Miracle

'Some 20 years ago I managed a launderette in Chelsea, London. I sometimes worked until 11.00 p.m., checking the till and various other things. At about 10.00 p.m. this one night I had locked the back door where the boiler-room was, and locked the front door to the shop. The boiler-room was approximately 28 feet from my counter, and the front door was about 30 feet away. It was possible for me to see the King's Road from the counter, but not the back door as there was a dividing door in-between. If someone had screamed outside at the back I would not have heard them, and to be heard from the front you would have to shout extremely loudly.

'It was a lovely and quiet evening, serenely so, in fact, when a voice said my name, "Glenda", very clearly, not loud but loud enough for me to twist round and answer, "Yes?"

'I cannot tell you if the voice was a lady's or a man's. I checked every place in the launderette to see if there was anyone there, but there wasn't.

'The next day at work the steam-press had packed up, so I took the plugs apart to check it. To cut this short, I had picked up one of the wires which was plugged into a socket in the boiler-room … but I was standing in water, not a good move. The next thing I felt was the live shock going through my body. Some minutes later I found myself 12 feet away by the door, where I presume the force had thrown me. Was I hurt? No!

'For me to have landed by the door with no physical injury was a miracle. I missed a huge water tank and a concrete boiler when I flew through the air … In fact, it was impossible because of the way they were positioned. I will leave it up to you to decide if the voice and my miracle escape are connected … but for me I think it has to be a yes!'

– Glenda, England

6

The Real Magic of Childhood

'There is a garden in every childhood, an enchanted place where colours are brighter, the air softer, and the morning more fragrant than ever again.' – Elizabeth Lawrence

I was delighted to have the opportunity of writing my book *Angel Kids* (also published by Hay House). Over the years I had collected many hundreds of stories of children who experienced paranormal phenomena in their lives and who were themselves psychic. *Angel Kids* was written as a resource for parents of psychic children, and also an exciting way of sharing the psychic encounters of children – after all, psychic children become psychic adults!

It seems unbelievable, but this phenomenon is real. Many 'imaginary friends' are in fact spirit visitors – visitors the children can see and interact with. Invisible to the parents and other adults, but they still exist just the same.

Children's psychic experiences are some of the most exciting because in their innocence they happily share what they have seen, felt or heard without prejudice. Very young children don't have the embarrassment that adults might … they probably don't realize that seeing spirit energies is unusual! Children encounter a wide range of phenomena which is normal for them. Some can hear the thoughts of others (telepathy); some young children seem to have the ability to perceive guardian angels or their spiritual guides; a favourite amongst the parents is when children are able to connect to their deceased relatives … especially when the children pass on messages from the afterlife. Our children can be mini-mediums!

Here are some of their stories and letters.

Reading Auras and Seeing 'Beautiful Nanny'

'I have just finished reading your *Angel Kids* book (which was amazing … and I read it quicker than any book I've ever read any book before – four days!).

'After reading the stories in the book I decided to write to you about my daughter Mia. Mia is almost eight and has always had trouble sleeping; she is sometimes terrified and often wakes up with "nightmares". Sometimes she says there is "another me in my bed with me". Mia can never get to sleep on her own and always hides under the covers. I have been trying out the tips in your book and they really help.

'She is very sensitive. One day I was driving while Mia and her brother Max were chatting away in the back of the car. Suddenly Mia started to talk about "Nanny Old" (Max called her "Nanny Old" because there are several elderly relatives in the family and she was the oldest, their great-grandmother).

'Max said to Mia, "What do you know about Nanny Old,

you've never even met her?" (He was right, she died when Mia was a couple of weeks old.) Mia then got very cross with him (she was about three at the time), and insisted that of course she knew her and that she was very beautiful. What came next made me laugh because Max, who was then six, said, "Well, that proves you've never met her, then, because Nanny Old was certainly not beautiful!" (She was in her 80s when she died!)

'I thought what Mia had said was an odd thing to say, but then realized that she may have had a visit from her great-grandmother, as I know that deceased loved ones can appear younger and in their prime of life when they visit us.

'Then just a few months ago Mia woke up one morning and saw her brother's aura. Without having any idea what it was, she said simply, "Wow, Max, your aura looks amazing today!"

'I was quite taken aback as I have never talked about that kind of thing with her and I have no idea how she knows the word "aura". Curious, I asked her and she said, "Oh, it's just that stuff around him, you know!"'

– Louise, England

You may be wondering who the 'other me' was in bed with little Mia – when we sleep at night our spirit separates from the body ... and often goes on its own adventures (yes, really). Clairvoyants can sometimes see this other 'me' floating around the body ... this is the part of us that has 'out-of-body' experiences. My daughter used to float over the top of her body every night when she was younger, and many of my readers have done this, too.

Here's another little girl who seems to see relatives from the other side of life. How do they do this? I love to think that our relatives and friends in the afterlife are watching over us, too.

My Other Mummy

'I first noticed the strange reactions when my daughter Janelle was around 20 months old. One night she woke me to ask, "Can you see Amy [a friend] there?" She pointed to the sky and said, "Amy came to visit me." I just acknowledged that I could see Amy, although in reality I could not.

'Then around the same time, we had a break-in during the night while we were sleeping. Although it was a frightening experience, fortunately we were not harmed. The burglars moved around the house going through cupboards, taking what they wanted while we slept through the whole ordeal.

'Two nights after the burglary, my daughter was in her bedroom, chatting to someone I couldn't see. I entered her room and asked her whom she was talking to and her immediate reaction was: Grandma Lilly. Now, the weird part is that my grandma, whom we called by this name, passed away about 10 years ago. I never mentioned the name to my little girl and I don't even have a picture of her. I loved her dearly, though, and she was always close to me.

'As recently as three months ago, I was driving along in the car one night with my daughter, now three and a half, and her friend. The two of them were sitting in the back seat of my car and all of a sudden my daughter was telling her friend that she'd once had another mummy, and then she went on to describe a family, complete with names and even a dog.

'Janelle went into detail about how they lived, and then she ended her story with, "but she's now living with her current mummy and the current mummy is very good and kind and is the right mummy for her." Janelle's friend had no clue as to how to react, and then started talking about school and tangible

things. I spoke to Janelle's therapist who said that maybe she does recall a previous life and can see things and speak to "dead" people. She's very good with animals and even pets "wild" animals.'
– Almarie, South Africa

How fantastic that Janelle has a therapist who completely understands these things!

Janelle is not alone – children all over the world recall their previous lives, although sadly they often forget their experiences when they get a little older. There are several books on the subject if you are interested in learning more. Check out your local bookshop or library for suggestions.

If you have a child in your family who recalls such things, do write the experiences down so that the family have a record – some experts on this phenomenon have tracked down previous families who existed exactly as the young child recalls … isn't that amazing?

Here is another letter, this time from a teenager.

Teen Spirit

'My name is Jade and I love your books. Sometimes the stories make me cry and sometimes they make me laugh. I would like to tell you two of my own experiences; one is just a very small story but it meant a lot to me at the time.

'I was sitting in my bedroom and I'd just finished reading your book *An Angel Held My Hand* (such a lovely book), and then I thought to myself, "I wonder if my angels have sent me a sign before but I just haven't noticed?" I asked them to send me another sign and this time I was ready and knew I wouldn't miss knowing that they were around me.

'As I walked onto the landing I noticed my sister's perfume bottle was sitting on the landing right under my feet … I was the only one in the house at the time, so no one could have placed it there, and I didn't remember it being on the landing when I went into my room earlier. The funniest thing was that the perfume was called "Angel". It made me giggle, anyway.

'The other experience is about a little girl who lived in my house many years before. She was quite a bit younger than me (I am 15 and she is/was about 13–14) and appears as a spirit. I'm sure it's her who plays around with things in my room.

'I have a little alarm clock which is decorated with the TV character Bagpuss the cat. The alarm should only go off if someone presses a button, but it never went off when it was set. However, whenever I was in my room the little girl would let me know she was there too by turning the alarm on. Sometimes when I wasn't in my room and the little girl needed me she would set the alarm off, and I would go up to my room to check. The alarm clock would then cut out even if it was in the middle of ringing! My mum thought the whole thing was great and none of us was scared.

'In the end we took the batteries out of the clock and placed them in the bin. Then one night when I was asleep I was actually woken up by the sound of the alarm clock. I was amazed because I checked the clock and Mum hadn't replaced the batteries!'
– Jade, England

This next story comes from Australia. Following a sad loss, a special grandma comes back to say hello to her living relatives.

Nanny in the Garden

'I believe that my cousin's three-year-old daughter Jill has seen an angel. My aunty passed away last March. It was very quick and unexpected, so it was hard for the family. She was such a family person and loved children. My cousin (my aunt's daughter) had two children of her own, including Jill who was aged only three at the time. We never told Jill that her Nanny had died, because she was too young to understand.

'Shorty afterwards Jill started saying she could see her Nanny, which was spooky. One day she told my cousin she could "see Nanny in the garden". She told us that Nanny said, "she's fine but misses us!"

'My cousin found it strange because she hadn't even told her daughter that her Nanny had died, so why would she come out with something like this? Jill even told us what her Nanny was wearing; when my cousin asked her, she replied "orange jumper and black trousers" … that's what she was buried in, but Jill couldn't have known that!

'The little one continues to see her Nanny, and recently told us that Nanny was in the swimming pool!'
– Karen, Australia

Spirits do often come back to see us wearing the clothes they were buried in … if it helps with proof. But they are just as likely to pick a favourite outfit from their earthly wardrobe. Sometimes the deceased turn up in a long white gown … angelic-like! Of course none of this explains why this little one was talking to a deceased Nanny she didn't know had died who was wearing the outfit she was buried in!

In this next story, it sounds to me like the little boy's guardian angel was on hand.

Car Park Terror

'One day I was driving to daycare to pick up my daughter. I had my six-year-old son Kevin in the car with me. He was busy playing with his Gameboy so when I got close to the daycare centre and started to turn into the parking lot, he apparently wasn't paying attention. Kevin swung the door open to get out but we were still on the road. As I carried on driving – not realizing at first what had happened – Kevin seemed to be somehow holding on to the door.

'I don't know where I got the strength to not panic. If I had I would have slammed on the brakes and he would probably have been thrown on the road or even underneath the car. I truly think there was an angel helping to guide me on what to do next.

'As soon as I realized what had happened I slowly put on the brakes and stopped the car. When I got out of the car and ran over to Kevin's side, I looked at the door and I just couldn't see anywhere that it would have been possible for him to hold on to the bottom of the door the way he had. There was absolutely nothing there he could have held on to.

'Terrified, I rushed to my son's side. Kevin was fine, other than his jeans which were torn a little on the bum where he had dragged along the road. He was completely fine except for a few little scratches. What a relief!

'I believe we both had angels with us that day: one to help me stay calm and stop the car in the safest possible way, and another one to hold on to my son and protect him. Thank you, angels.'

– Janice, Canada

Janice's story is terrifying … what a narrow escape little Kevin had that day. Not only do I believe that we all have guardian angels, but I feel that we also have spiritual guides watching over us and guiding us along our life path. Who is it that this next little boy sees, do you think?

The Man

'I want to tell you the story of my son Nathan, who had psychic experiences when he was two-and-a-half and then four years old. It was the time that we were building an extension to our house, and we closed the old doorway to our kitchen and made a new opening for the new kitchen. My son Nathan was then just about two-and-a-half years of age, but a very smart boy with an advanced ability to speak.

'In his bedroom there is a staircase that leads up to the attic and, one afternoon after getting him out of bed after his nap, Nathan said to me, "Mummy, do you see that man too who is sitting at the top of the stairs?" I replied that I did not see him but asked my son what he looked like and what he was doing. My son said he didn't know what he was doing there, but as he told me I could see that Nathan was not scared or even wondering about it.

'I have a friend who is able to do channelling with her guides (psychically receive messages and answers to questions) and I called her to ask if she could get more information about this. Soon we knew it had something to do with the extension and the doorway that was closed. The spirit seemed to have lost his way and couldn't find the new doorway, so he was searching for information. My friend also told me to talk to him, even though I couldn't see him. She told me to burn some pure incense sticks in my son's room and to tell the spirit what we were doing, and that it was OK. We also told him that, if he wanted, he could go towards the light.

'Well although this was all new to me and seemed a little strange, it did seem to work and it all went quiet for a while.

'One evening when Nathan was about four, he told me the man had returned. We had a daughter by then, too, and my son was sitting by the changing table in their room. The table stood very close to the staircase. I asked him again what the man was doing, and this time Nathan said he was holding two little lights in his hands. I asked what the man meant by the lights, and Nathan said there was one for me and one for him. Then he said we had to reach out and take the light into our hands, so I decided to give it a go. When I wasn't reaching in the exact direction, Nathan even said to me that I had to reach higher. He also took a light in his hand. Then I asked what we were supposed to do with them. Nathan told me I had to hold the light against my heart and he had to do the same. So we did. And then the spirit left.

'Nathan was not scared; in fact he was so convinced that I did not doubt for any second that everything he said was true. Again I called my friend for a channelling, and now she got the message that the spirit was very grateful to us for showing him that we appreciated him and believed in his appearance. He also told us that it is his honour to protect our house and to keep us safe.

'Nathan is now nine years of age, and is a truly loving, giving, intelligent boy who is always concerned about other people's wellbeing. He sometimes tells me he has the ability to see things happen just before they do. One time he warned me, when I had to go out in my car, to be very careful with a turn I had to take. I was holding his words in mind and, about two minutes later, I had to take a turn and a car was driving on my side of the road. Luckily I was driving very slowly and I was able to avoid an accident. Nathan also can see the energy that is in and around mandalas [mandala means "sacred circle"; it's a colour healing tool used for divination and meditation, and dates back to ancient times]. Nathan can actually see them swirling and turning in the most beautiful colours.

'It is truly an amazing experience and an honour to have such a person in our lives. Luckily my husband and I are very open to the "other world". We always have had people around us who are "gifted" and we are always looking out for little subtle signs from the other side. Lately I realize that my own dreams also have messages from the other side, too – we are all more aware than we know if only we open ourselves up to the messages.

'I'm happy to see that the world is becoming more and more open so that love, the greatest power, can flow into it! Many greetings from us all, and thank you for bringing this subject into the world!'

– Debora, Belgium

I love these stories of our special children. So many children being born into the world today appear wise beyond their years, and are very knowing, beautiful souls with great intelligence and an enlightened way of looking at the world … being psychic is so natural to them. They seem to use abilities which most of us are not even aware of. You just know when strangers look into the pram and say, ' … he's been here before …', they're right!

Checking Out His Grandson

'My father Raymond suffered from bowel cancer 27 years ago; he suffered terrible pain and the cancer spread to his spine. I was pregnant during his illness, and he asked if I would name the baby, if I had a son, Raymond. Two months later my darling father passed away, and we were all devastated.

'After my father left, the night he died my mother and my auntie both heard footsteps pass the bedroom door to go downstairs. For a long time while he was still alive he'd had to sleep on his own because of the pain, and he'd wait 'til everybody would retire for the night before going downstairs to sleep on the sofa. Mum heard his footsteps at his usual time.

'When our baby was born we did indeed call him Raymond, just as my father had requested. The night Raymond was christened I was wide awake and Raymond was asleep in his cot. I was lying facing the door, and standing there was my wonderful father. He looked well, like he used to before he was ill. He was wearing his best coat but he had no legs! Then he was over by Raymond's cot and looked into it to see my son. It was an amazing experience and I felt so peaceful, it was a lovely feeling. I felt so happy and contented that I drifted off into a deep sleep.'

– Glenys, Wales

7

Animals Are Angels Too

'Animals are such agreeable friends – they ask no questions, they pass no criticisms' – **George Eliot**

Strangely, some people are under the illusion that science knows and understands everything that happens in our world … it doesn't. We are discovering new things about the animal kingdom all the time. I thought you might enjoy a few stories about the extraordinary animals among us. If we don't know everything there is to know about this world, then how can we be sure that other things such as angels don't exist around us? I hope this chapter might open your eyes a little (it certainly did mine).

UNKNOWN SPECIES

A jumping spider, three new types of tree frog, and a gecko with stripes are amongst a selection of more than 50 new species which have recently been found in Papua New Guinea, according to Conservation International, the environmental group. A tiny mouse has been discovered living in mountain forests high up in the Andes recently, too. These animals are ones we can see with our naked eye, beings who live at the same 'vibration' that we do … yet even they have remained hidden for so long.

Of course it's more than likely that there are many more life-forms which share the same vibration as air or gases, creatures that we can't see with the naked eye. I can't wait for better evidence of the mysterious giant ape species 'Big Foot' (Sasquatch). These hidden species have been witnessed for many years but no one will believe for sure they exist until we have captured one. They have been spotted mainly in forests in America's Pacific Northwest.

Another one of these mysterious creatures is the red-eyed chupacabra, witnessed by many in Puerto Rico. This terrifying creature is known as 'the goat sucker' and has been blamed for many animal deaths. Many folk have witnessed the creature, but it too has never been caught. Some say the chupacabra has been seen swooping through the treetops, and others say the creature has huge hairy monkey-like arms, a snake-like tongue and spines which look like wings! No doubt time will explain all.

Years ago fishermen were laughed at when they described terrifying sea monsters with eyes the size of plates, yet we now know that the giant squid not only exists but that the female of the species can grow to be up to 10 metres! Photographs of the giant squids on Goshiki Beach in Japan were taken in 2002. There are reports of squid measuring up to 20 metres long, but no official records exist on this … yet! It seems like the ancient fishermen were correct after all.

Another strange creature has been spotted around New Jersey since 1735. Over 2,000 people have witnessed a creature known locally as 'The Jersey Devil'. As with many other weird creatures, sightings still continue to this day, and whenever the animal is spotted locally it causes mass panic, with schools and businesses temporarily closing down. One observer described the being as having a very long tail that narrows at the ends, and horns, and feet which were a little like hooves!

If these strange creatures (with many witnesses) are still a mystery to us, doesn't it seem likely that angels and 'light-beings', which have been seen for many thousands of years, are also real and also (for good reason) resist capture by a camera lens or in their physical form? It certainly makes you wonder, at any rate. I do consider that maybe these creatures aren't always in our realm … maybe they exist in more than one dimension and appear and readily disappear when they need to. There certainly doesn't seem to be a shortage of witnesses, at least.

HEALING CREATURES

Any pet owner will tell you about the comfort a pet can bring, especially for the lonely. But did you know there was a more scientific explanation behind the healing abilities of our pets?

Cat Healing

Cats seem to have an intuition about when we are feeling unwell. My own pets love to snuggle up with me, and are always close by when I feel under the weather. If you have a cold, your cat wants to wrap itself round your head. Tummy ache and the cat lies on your lap … they just know where you need the healing.

We know that a cat's purr is relaxing and seems to help with stress, but science has proved that your cat's purr produces a vibration that is helpful in healing. A study by Elizabeth von Muggenthaler (a bio-acoustic specialist at the Fauna Communication Research Institute in North Carolina) discovered that a cat purrs within the range of 25–40 cycles per second (Hz). Amazingly, exposure to 20–50 Hz frequencies helps relieve pain and heals muscles, tendons, ligaments and bones in both humans … and cats; they are therapeutic frequencies. Maybe this is why cats know when we are unwell – they literally feel it. Hug a cat today!

Dog Healing

Dogs, too, are our loving companions and healers, the faithful friends of humankind. They guard us, guide us, love us unconditionally and even act as working dogs on farms, and in service (sniffer dogs, guide dogs for the blind, and healing pets visiting hospitals and retirement homes, etc.).

SAVING LIVES

Dramatic stories of pets saving lives are always appearing in the news, but dogs and cats are not the only heroes! Here are three stories about our heroic feathered friends.

Chatterbox Parrot Saves the Day

Recently Willie, a Quaker parrot, was awarded a 'Lifesaver' award by his local Red Cross. When babysitter Megan Howard left the room for a few moments, Hannah, the toddler she was taking care of, began to choke on her breakfast cereal. Clever Willie began squawking 'Mama … baby' and flapping his wings, which alerted Megan.

When she returned to the room the young child was already turning blue, but Megan was able to perform the Heimlich manoeuvre, which dislodged the object from the child's throat just in time. The bird's call for help literally saved the toddler's life.

Cockatiel Alarm

Brian Molineux, a 72-year-old night porter, was taken ill at his Essex home and collapsed on the floor after having a stroke. His 17-year-old bird immediately began making a terrible racket. The bird has access to the whole house, and Brian later told reporters that he always fed the bird each morning … but not that morning, as Brian had collapsed before he'd been able to perform his morning routine.

Did the bird want feeding or did it just make 'a heck of a noise' because it knew its owner was in danger? Mrs Molineux was still in bed at the time, but was alerted by the bird's squawking and she rushed downstairs to see what was the matter. Prompt action meant that Mr Molineux was able to make a full recovery from his stroke; both owners credit their bird with saving Brian's life!

Dog Angel

Dogs can be trained to recognize illness in their owners. Chushla, a bedlington-whippet cross, has saved her owner from a diabetic attack … over and over again. This is one of many stories I've come across in newspapers and internet reports.

Clever Chushla literally smells the subtle change in body odour when her owner's blood sugar levels drop to dangerously low levels. Elizabeth Wilkinson has diabetes and Chushla will alert her owner to a possible onset of an attack, as many as three times a week. The pet can literally stop the mum-of-three from falling into a coma and dying. A real doggie Earth-angel.

NOT JUST A LOT OF MONKEY BUSINESS

Boy, do we humans think we have all the answers – but animals can be so clever. I was delighted to read about more than 30 chimps in the Congo basin who have been using sticks to gather honey. Although chimps in other areas have used tools in the past, this seems to be a new method which is exclusive to this particular bunch. The group was filmed by conservation specialists who witnessed the chimps using up to five different types of stick to achieve their goal.

Orang-utans are a bright lot, too and their antics are often written about in the press. Just this week I read about Suryia the orang-utan and his 'pet dog' Roscoe! The two are the best of friends and live at a 50-acre preserve at Myrtle Beach, South Carolina. Suryia walks her 'pet' around on his lead, and the two particularly like swimming together! Apparently Roscoe is perfectly happy receiving her hugs from an orang-utan. As I write this the two are just about to appear on *Oprah* together (I'm not kidding)!

In another news item this week, an orang-utan escaped from a zoo in Australia by short-circuiting an electric fence, piling up debris at the edge of her cage and then climbing out. Apparently the naughty ape changed her mind after only a short time and returned to her cage … but she's tried to outsmart keepers in the past. Karta is a 27-year-old female orang-utan, and shows us just how bright these creatures really are.

Then there is Bonnie, a 32-year-old female orang-utan who can whistle … yes, really. Apparently the keepers at the Smithsonian National Zoo, where she lives, say she taught herself!

… SOMETHING FISHY GOING ON? DON'T COUNT ON IT!

It seems that even fish are not as dumb as we make them out to be. The mosquitofish, an American freshwater fish named after its favourite titbit, has been studied extensively by scientists who've discovered that it can count.

In other recent laboratory experiments the fish were trained inside a tank to go through an underwater door which took them into a compartment which enabled them to join the rest of their group. The 'right' doors had specific geometric shapes on them, and the fish picked the same door over and over again, even when the shapes varied in size and colour.

While we're on the subject … rhesus macaque monkeys, studied by scientists at Duke University, have been found to be able to subtract, using tests placed on a screen in front of them. Wonders will never cease.

DOG AIRLINES

Proof that some people are beginning to realize animals are important in our world, too: one airline has been created which caters exclusively for our furry friends. The very first pooch passengers fly out from a tiny airport outside of New York. Pet Airways was set up specifically to provide a safe solution for pet transportation (which also includes cats). Of course the pets don't actually have to strap themselves into a seat; kennels are secured to special shelves inside the plane before they are taken comfortably to their new destination. Today New York … tomorrow … the world!

THE WORLD AS WE KNOW IT

OK, I'll admit it, this little chapter was a fun diversion, but I wanted to open your eyes to the world around us. We take animals for granted, assume we are the Earth's true supreme leaders and are assured that we know the truth of everything and expect science to know the answer to every question. We're not, we don't … and it doesn't.

We can't even begin to fathom the animal kingdom let alone stretch outside of our comfort zone and consider other possibilities for life. It's time for us to wake up! Life exists for us in a bubble – who the heck knows what's outside of that …?

MYSTERIOUS ANIMAL ANTICS

Many of my readers have experienced mysterious afterlife contact with animals after they have passed over. Our pets survive physical death as we do and, like human souls, long to let us know that they are OK.

When Maureen and her family adopted their fun-loving Jack Russell, Tag, as a puppy, they had years' worth of companionship. So strong were the bonds of love that Tag continued to spend time with them … even after death!

Life After Life for a Dog Named Tag

'I was living in England, near Leicester, when we adopted Tag. My husband Dave knew a farmer with some puppies, and when we went over to the farm, it turned out that Tag was the last pup left.

'She was curled up in a cat basket all alone. Her face was so lost and dejected … lonely for her brothers and sisters, I guessed … but she immediately melted my heart. She was adorable and right away I knew we would take her home with us.

'Our children Andrew (15), Adam (12) and Kirsty (10) welcomed Tag with open arms, and Dave and I fell in love with her immediately, but we weren't too sure how our other pets would cope with the newcomer. Alex the cat stayed away at first, but soon got used to this bouncy stranger. Toby, our other Jack Russell, was also a bit wary of her initially but eventually they became firm friends.

'Tag was a bit of a monkey! She was always digging at molehills in the local fields and she loved chasing rabbits given half a chance. Tag was a loyal and affectionate dog, and whenever I'd been out for the day she was always ready to greet me at the door, tail wagging. Tag was so excited she used to have a sort of grin on her face … which strangers have interpreted as a snarl. It wasn't: Tag always greeted her friends with her happy, smiley face!

'Tag was a big fan of chewy toys but they never lasted long, especially the rope ones. Tag could demolish a chew toy in days. One of her favourite things was lying out in the sunshine, but unlike most dogs she hated getting wet, so bath-time was always a challenge! She used to shiver so much, and always looked sad. We felt so sorry for her.

'When Tag was two years old, we had her mated. Everything went well right up to the birth. During labour she got into difficulties and I had to rush her to the vets. We were terrified that we might lose her, but the vet was brilliant and she pulled through. Tragically, three of the pups died, but they did manage to save one. Tag now had a daughter and we called her Brambles. Naturally we kept our miracle puppy and she soon began to thrive!

'Years later I remember a terrifying experience when the dogs disappeared under a fence. At the time I'd been working at our local stables, and while I was at work Dave took Tag and Brambles out for a walk. We'd arranged that he would meet me after my shift ended, but he was late and I was really starting to worry. Eventually Dave arrived and explained that he'd been searching for our escape artists, who'd disappeared during their walk. We now searched the lanes together, but it soon started to get dark and very cold, and eventually we had to call off the search. We were both devastated and had a sleepless night worrying about what had happened to our special friends.

'Early the next morning we started looking for the dogs again. In desperation I phoned round the local dog homes. The police station even joined in the hunt and made posters with the dogs' photographs on, and posted them all around the neighbourhood. Even the local kids helped us to look for Tag and Brambles … we searched night after night, and eventually I feared the worst. I just cried and cried, knowing our special friends had probably gone forever.

'About a week later, I was at work when my husband called me. The dogs had been found! He'd gone for one last look in the place where we'd lost them … Brambles was spotted in the field with Tag behind her. Tag had lost so much weight that Dave had to carry her home. I was in such a flap that my boss let me go home right away. I couldn't wait to be reunited with my faithful friends.

'I was shocked when I walked in the door. My healthy, happy pets were now skinny and filthy dirty. The local vets treated them for dehydration, but apart from a little loss in weight the two were OK. We never did find out what happened to them, but we suspect that rabbit holes might have had something to do with it! I've always wondered how they had managed without food or water for a whole week!

'That night Tag slept in my bed with me. I wasn't about to let her out of my sight. For a long time she used to follow me everywhere, even when I went into the bathroom. She would only eat her dinner if I was with her. Our separation made us closer than ever after her disappearance, and a sixth sense developed between us. Tag always knew when I was sad or upset. She would shove her face into mine and try to lick my face as if to say, "I'm here for you." She just knew when I needed comforting.

'Tag was a special dog and we had many more years together. But when she was 10 she suddenly started to lose weight. At first we thought it was due to dental problems. She had really bad breath and had stopped eating her food. We took her to the vets and were distraught when we discovered she had severe kidney failure. Nothing more could be done. It was her time. We were heartbroken. Tag had been a constant companion, a family member, and now we had to have her put to sleep. The hardest decision that an owner ever has to make ...

'Tag was cremated. We planned to bury her ashes in the garden where she used to lie in the sun, but that night it soon became clear that something strange was going on. Brambles couldn't settle, and kept growling and pacing back and forth in the room with her hackles up. She was sensing or seeing something in the room that we couldn't. Had Tag's spirit followed us home? We couldn't be sure ... but later we knew she had.

'When Tag was alive she always barked out a high-pitched yelp ... almost a scream, whenever the telephone rang. That night we were snuggled up together on the settee watching TV when the phone rang. The usual noise could be heard by my feet and without thinking, Dave said, "Quiet dog!" But of course, Tag was gone … Then my eyes met Dave's as we both realized what we'd heard. Startled, we both said together, "That's Tag!"

'Since then we've both felt Tag jumping on the bed in the same way she used to do when she was alive. She was a dog full of character, emotion, fun and love. She's totally irreplaceable … unique, and I will miss her always, but I do take great comfort in knowing that she comes back to visit us every now and again.'

– Maureen, Scotland

Our pets have a magical connection with us while they are still on this side of life, too. My cats never leave my side if I am at home, and follow me from room to room. As I type this my large ginger tom cat is almost sitting on the keyboard (and strangely, later as I edit this same section he is right here again). It sometimes feels like they are helping me with my work.

On occasion I feel my cats are sleeping on my bed at night – although I know their physical bodies are downstairs in the conservatory and kitchen where we shut them in for the night; yet during the night they are with me in a spiritual sense.

Donna's experience is similar to my own.

Cats Love Angels, Too

'Last February my Nan passed away. We were driving to London to bury her; we had the funeral flowers in the back of the car. All of sudden another car hit us. It was totally unexpected and we were all very shocked.

'I've heard people say their lives flash past their eyes, and this is what happened to me. I know this sounds really strange, but while I was having this experience the being that came to me was my cat Pixie, who isn't dead (thank God). It was like she "astrally projected" to my location to protect me! I could see her so clearly.

'The car was a write-off and I was a nervous wreck, but knowing that Pixie was with me during the experience was a real comfort … although I have no idea how this might have happened. We were already in a fragile state, but to be in a car accident on the way to a funeral – it seems unreal!

'Pixie is three years old and a very clever cat. The only time she stays in my room is when I'm reading my angel books. Strange as it sounds, when I don't have an angel book and I'm reading something else Pixie goes to another room to sleep. Perhaps there is more to Pixie that meets the eye!'
– Donna, England

Perhaps there is! Here is another cat story.

Best Friends
'When I was nine years old my mum brought a Blue Birman cat and we became the best of friends. She followed me everywhere, slept in my bed when I was sleeping, sat next to me at the dinner table and stayed with me when I played with my toys.

'We had her for about five years or so, until one day we found her very ill. We rushed her to the vets and she was there for a few days and not improving. I remember the phone ringing and the vet on the line speaking to my mum. Mum then came

into my room and all she said was, "… I'm sorry, sweetheart."
At that moment I knew my precious cat had not made it. I was
absolutely devastated. No one in my family had passed away
and this was the first death I'd had to deal with. It was very hard,
as we'd been such good friends.

'Just as I was dropping off to sleep that night, I spotted my
precious cat sitting by the bedroom door. She walked straight up
to my bed, sat down and just watched me. As I was so young I
didn't know what to do and was pretty frightened. My brother
then walked down the hallway past my door and the cat slowly
disappeared.

'To this day I still think of what happened and I know she
was coming to say goodbye. At least I knew she was no longer
in pain.'
– Samantha, Australia

I've read many stories of dogs and cats coming back from the other
side, but what about hamsters? This owner certainly believes this
can happen.

Comfort from a Hamster

'I once owned a Russian dwarf hamster called Elgar. I had him
for over a year after my Nan passed away and he eased the pain
of bereavement for me; it really helped.

Then in January 2009 I noticed that he had a lump on his
little body, so I took him to the vets. I think that deep in my heart
I knew what it was; I think every pet owner has a sense of these
things. The vet confirmed it: he had cancer.

'Elgar was a right little fighter, but the tumour got so big and I
felt so sad for him. Our souls were connected on all levels and I

was praying to my angels and God for them to heal him; maybe that was why he survived so long, I don't know!

'Then there came a point when I had to make the awful decision to have my baby hamster put down. I was totally heartbroken and cried a lot. Everything seemed to remind me of Elgar. I was at the vets and was with him when the vet put him to sleep. I was sobbing so much that even the vet was choked up. People might think it silly, but I loved Elgar so much, even though to everyone else he was "just" a hamster.

'After I buried him I decided to have a rest. I was just dropping off to sleep when all of a sudden I felt his little hands on my index finger; I could picture him so clearly in my mind and I just burst into tears again. This time, though, I knew he was OK in his new form and would still be around me.

'Even after all this time I do sense him sometimes. Pets of all kinds are so special. It's wonderful to know that, like humans, they continue after death, too.'

– Donna, England

What about the connection between horses and humans? Horses have been faithful companions and servants for humankind for many years. That special trust which connects us both is never broken. This lady also had an earlier spirit encounter, so I have left her email intact so that you can also enjoy her ghostly encounter as she told it to me.

Spirit Visits and Horse Galloping

'Hello. I bought your books hoping for some answers to what happened to me last year. We own a static caravan on the east coast of England, right at the cliff's edge.

'One night in September we went to bed and I was woken by what I thought was my husband standing at the end of my bed. I looked up and thought it was my husband going to the toilet, as he was standing where the door is. After lying back down but not hearing any movement I decided to look back and, this time, as I tried to sit myself up my leg touched my husband, still asleep at my side. This really shocked me!

'Now looking back to the foot of my bed I could see a gentleman in what I thought was a naval uniform. He did not look at me or move and he had one arm held out, holding a cane, and he was looking straight ahead. He must have been there a good few minutes and I found I was now surprised but I did not feel scared at all. Then he gently floated upwards, all the room lit up with movement like the sea waves.

'As he disappeared the room went very dark; I have blackout curtains up as the nearby lighthouse used to light up the room, so it's totally black, but he really lit up the whole caravan with his glowing figure.

'I woke up my husband and told him what I'd seen but he does not believe me even though I was covered in goosebumps. For the rest of the night I was in tears and I felt so much sorrow for this man, and even now it brings tears to my eyes thinking of the sadness I felt at this time.

'Just last month in the same bed I was woken up by a bright light again; it was so bright just like you have when a camera flash goes off in your eyes and when you close your eyes you still see the light. This light came nearer and nearer until it was just above my head, when I could really see what it was. It was a boat's propeller; it was turning and I could see the sea flowing through it and foaming up. This time I woke my husband but as he was waking it floated up to the ceiling and broke up, causing the room to go dark again. He says I was covered in goosebumps again, but no sad feelings were associated with this second visit.

'If anyone was to tell me I would see a ghost I would be so scared, but I did not feel afraid. Actually I felt so privileged, and look forward to the next time if I am to be so lucky again.

'I have no answers as to who this gentleman is or why he came to visit. [Note from Jacky: I immediately picked up a story of this seaman who drowned. His sadness was immense as he realized he would never return to the family he loved or be able to let anyone know what had happened to him.]

'After reading your books it made me remember back over 10 years ago when I had to have my horse put down. It broke my heart and I was in a right mess that night. In the middle of the night my son, who was just under two years old, woke me and my husband up because he was shouting in his sleep, "horses galloping!"

'We looked at each other and could not believe what he'd said. Usually when he was talking about the horse he never said "horses" but "popos". I don't think he even knew what "galloping" was! I am sure it was Goldie (my horse) letting me know he was fine now. Goldie was 21 and was on steroids for his breathing, which weakened his bones. On the day we had him put to sleep his front foreleg broke and he could not move. Knowing that he was galloping once again brought us all immense comfort.'

– Amanda, England

ANIMALS BRING SIGNS

A regular theme through many of my books is animals and birds who appear in mysterious ways to bring signs from our loved ones on the other side of life:

- **Butterflies are a traditional sign of 'spirit' presence. They are a regular signal in people's lives. It's amazing how many butterflies get trapped in funeral cars. Watch out also for moths and dragonflies.**
- **When you're feeling sad at the loss of a loved one, a regular bird visitor to your garden is very comforting … is the bird letting you know that your loved one is OK?**
- **Dogs will bark and wag their tails at unseen visitors … a spirit, maybe?**
- **Cats, too, seem to see things we cannot. My cats have even been known to run away from 'nothing' (well, I can't see it anyway!).**

Here is Linda's story and, as before, there is a mixed bag of experiences here … I've hope you enjoy them, too!

Love Is Like a Butterfly – and Other Things …

'I have been attempting to research the phenomenon of butterflies, out of interest, to see if I could find a solution to something that happened to me. A few years ago I was going through a really hard time and had just split from my partner, who was very abusive both physically and mentally. He wasn't just abusive to me but to the children also, and actually attacked my daughter and myself in front of my youngest son, who was only four at the time.

'One day I started to plan my escape in my head. I was a nervous wreck! I left my home and moved into an unfurnished flat with my three children with virtually nothing. We had no furniture and my family rallied round to get me the basics. What made matters worse was that I was pregnant when I left and I couldn't cope with another child in my mental state. Sadly I made the decision to terminate the pregnancy (this was a decision I did not take lightly and still feel very saddened by, but I know it was the right thing to do!).

'I found out a week later that my partner was having an affair and his girlfriend was also pregnant, which completely messed up my head. Soon after I started to get many signs that someone was watching over me. This was something that I had noticed before, but now these feelings were heightened.

'One beautiful sunny day I went out to hang out my washing and, to my amazement, there were hundreds of white butterflies fluttering around my washing line (one of those whirly things). As I attempted to hang out my washing the butterflies were diving towards me and I felt perhaps they were attracted to the washing because it was a white wash. As I hung it out I kept having to run away. As I looked around I noticed they were only around my line (with a few strays fluttering on the outskirts). I was amazed at how many there were, and found this very strange, but as there are a few trees around where we were living I felt maybe they had all hatched at the same time.

'I went back inside with a funny feeling, and when I came back there were none, no butterflies at all. It was a mystery but strangely comforting. I mentioned this to my neighbour and she hadn't noticed anything.

'Another unusual thing that happened to me was when I was getting ready to go into town. I had just brushed and washed my floors throughout my home. I kept hearing noises in my flat, footsteps and doors closing, etc., that morning, and felt that I wasn't alone. I went through to select my clothing for the day and I could hear a tapping sound coming from my sitting room. I went through and sat down to put on my shoes and, to my amazement, I saw a tiny pile of what turned out to be plaster from my mantelpiece (there were loose tiles). This little pile was very neat and tidy but also unexplainable, as the floor was still wet from mopping and I knew for a fact it hadn't been there before. I was also alone in the house, as the children were at school. I left with my stomach churning!

'I went to my bed another night and had just put my head down on the pillow when I could feel an icy blast of air around my face. It came on suddenly and lasted about two or three minutes. I sat up and looked around. My bedroom door and window were both closed. It continued to linger, then faded away.

'Another night I was woken in the early hours of the morning by a sound coming from the kitchen. I recognized the sound immediately: it was the wire spring door-stopper in the kitchen. Someone was "pinging" it loudly. I jumped up to check it out and it stopped immediately. I checked on my children and they were all in bed, but I'd known that even before I'd checked.

'I returned to bed and it started again. I put my foot out of the bed and it stopped again. I got back under the covers and just listened, and again it started. It stopped and I realized I had felt no fear; I felt watched over instead. I started to feel this was my deceased grandmother watching over me and letting me know she was around, though in life we hadn't been close due to family issues between the families when I was only small. I told my children of this the next day and they didn't believe me, but weeks later my daughter jumped into my bed terrified in the middle of the night after hearing the same noise.

'In the early hours of another night my phone was ringing. I jumped to answer in a panic, thinking that if anyone phones in the night it's most likely an emergency. When I picked up the phone there was no one there. I dialled 1471 and it was my own number that came up!

'Strange noises have come and gone – footsteps, the door knocking, doors opening and closing – though my children have also heard all of these at different times, including my sceptical son. And there are often smells that apparently only I can smell!

'Many things happened before I split from my ex and I even have stories from my childhood. I often feel that someone is sitting on my bed at night; I see dark figures at the end of my bed. One time I was dozing on the settee on my own, when I was about 17, and opening my eyes I saw a white mist in the form of a young man sitting on the arm of the chair looking at me. I looked on in amazement and it appeared to get up and walk towards me, but then faded away as it got closer. I felt calm but saddened.

'A strange thing once happened in the graveyard when I was still with my ex-partner. My children and I were visiting graves of the deceased that we knew. We were leaving my ex's uncle's grave when suddenly I saw a small bird flying straight for me. My ex and children also witnessed this. It flew directly at me, then lowered itself straight towards my feet. I stopped dead in fear that I would hurt it, because it flew straight between my legs and fluttered around my feet for a moment. I was stunned because, by nature, birds take flight as we approach, don't they? I wasn't sure but felt this to be a sign from my ex's uncle for some reason, although I can't be sure, but surely it was a sign of some sort?

'Very recently there was a bright green bird trying to get in my window. It looked like a canary but it was about four times the size, with beautiful orange and yellow markings. It really wanted to get in so I felt it might be a domesticated bird, and I tried in vain to get it to come through my window, tempting it with food, but as I have safety windows it was unable to figure out how to get in through the small gap. Though it did try!

'It sat outside my window in a tree 'til the next day, and eventually left because seagulls started to attack it. In the meantime I was phoning round to see if anyone had reported such a bird missing, as I was sure it would be sorely missed, but I came up with nothing. After it left there was nothing more to do other than find the whole affair strange. Then, about five weeks later, I saw the exact same bird on the TV and there was a report saying there was a small "colony" of about 4,000 of them down in the south of England, in one particular county though I can't remember where … these birds were indeed exotic. I was never sure if it was a sign or not …'

– Linda, Scotland

What a fascinating collection of experiences. Once you are aware of signs, it does open you up to more and more of them. Who's to say which of these were signs or not? Sometimes it really is down to individual interpretation, but I felt that Linda's experiences were worth sharing with you just the same.

Here is another bird-sign story that came via email.

Bird Messenger

'I've always had a belief that there is some sort of afterlife and the possibility of angels and the like. To put you in the picture, my wife passed over a few months ago and I have found it difficult, so I have been reading a few books, going to church, etc. I did feel I had angels around me, but I had no proof.

'I bought your book *Angels Watching Over Me* by chance when I was browsing. I only read a little in bed each night, so I haven't finished it yet, but I felt compelled to tell you about this experience. You know how you said in your book that some proof would be nice, like a certain bird appearing, in your case a blue tit? Well, this got me thinking: I have loads of most common birds, including tits, in my garden, so I thought, "Yes, why not? But it would have to be something very unusual to convince me, say a hawk-type of bird." I thought this would be out of the question and gave it no more thought.

'The very next afternoon I was mucking about with my computer when something caught my eye. I looked out of my window to see a hawk sitting about 4 feet from me on my veranda rail, looking in at me. Of course it immediately took off when it realized I was there. Well, I'd say the odds of that happening are about as good as winning the lottery! What more proof did I need that the afterlife is real? I'd say I had what I'd asked for, especially as I live in the middle of a village.

'Your book is certainly helping me come to terms with my loss.'

– Ken, England

Birds are very common signs, and I've written about them often … especially the unmistakable robin redbreast.

The Robin

'My mother passed on 12 years ago, at the age of 59. It was an awful shock to all of us as she was so fit and healthy and extremely young-looking. She was divorced from my father and used to go on holidays with other divorced and separated women friends. One Christmas, the year before she died, they all went to a hotel in Cornwall for a few days. Mum got up early one morning to walk in the hotel grounds, and a robin appeared to be following her as she walked. It stood still while she took a photograph of it, and she showed me the picture when we met up. That Christmas she gave me a gift, and the gift tag was a picture of a robin. After she died I discovered this gift tag in my home one day, so I kept it on a pine dresser that I had in my kitchen.

'About six months later I was talking to my daughter about my mum when the robin gift tag suddenly came off the dresser and landed at my feet. Since then, every time a robin appears we all say it's Mum coming to see us.

'Today I have been watching the Hillsborough memorial service (15th April). I spent my early childhood living very near the football ground where this tragedy happened and people lost their lives. Mum and I went to the ground the day after the disaster to lay flowers; so today was very emotional as I watched the memorial on TV because it also reminded me of Mum.

'Suddenly I thought I heard a noise at my window and, when I looked up, there was a robin on my garden wall looking through the window at me. It had its head cocked to one side

and was just staring at me. I was very emotional already, but this just put the icing on the cake and I cried before I said, "Hello, Mum" to the robin and it flew down to the garden and continued to look up at me. It was amazing and made me feel so good inside.'
– **Diana, Ireland**

There is so much more to our animal world. Pets in particular are very special to humankind. I thank God every day for the wonderful blessing of the love we share with our pets … on both sides of life.

8

Angels on Earth

'We are each other's angels, we meet when it is time.'
– Chuck Brodsky

EVERYONE CAN BE AN 'ANGEL'

After they have done a good deed we might say to someone, 'Oh, you are an angel.' Of course we mean that person has angelic qualities like kindness or maybe unconditional love. But is it possible for someone actually to be an angel on Earth? Would we even know if we were angels ourselves?

Creating kindness wherever you go is an important skill for life. We know that for good health and total wellbeing it's important to give as well as to receive. Helping others is actually good for you! So how can you help others? Consider it important 'pay-back' to spread a little happiness wherever you go.

Popping a few coins into a charity dish is not the same as litter-picking in your local neighbourhood. Making a monthly donation to 'Help the Aged' is important, but not as important as helping your elderly neighbour out with her shopping.

We know it's important to ask our angels for their help if we need it. Sometimes your angels are going to send human helpers to your aid. One day the angels may request *your* help – be ready to assist when the call comes. You'll know when this is: you'll get that certain 'tug' in your stomach, a 'gut feeling' – you may even feel guilty if you ignore the calling. I promise you, if you help whenever and wherever you are 'requested', that amazing feeling you get inside will let you know you did the right thing!

CONNECTING TO THE ANGELS ... SOME FUN TIPS AND IDEAS

Do you want to feel closer to your own guardian angels? Here are a few tips to get you started:

- Ask the angels to help you whenever you feel you need their help. Sometimes the most important thing is to know that you are not alone during your troubles. Finding a single white feather in an unusual place might be the perfect sign to comfort you. It's easy to handle any challenge if you know that others support you. Let your angels do this for you.
- Wearing a little symbol of your belief will act as a perfect reminder that the angels are around you. It's easy to find jewellery of all sorts: angel pins, angel necklaces and earrings are available in all sorts of designs, including those with precious and semi-precious stones. How about an angel coin to carry around in your purse?
- If jewellery isn't your thing, how about a bumper sticker for your car? Many new age shops and internet suppliers have these in many different designs. A declaration of 'I believe

in Angels' might just be perfect in the back window of your vehicle … and will remind you to ask the angels to watch over you when you're driving out and about.

- Angel pins are not expensive and make the perfect gifts for saying 'congratulations' on, for example, passing a driving test or exams, or as a little something to wear at your wedding, a christening or a funeral. The list is endless. Buy several when you see them and keep them in stock, ready for any occasion. The plainer ones make perfect tie-tacks, too.
- Even clothes have angel symbols and words on them now, especially children's clothes. Baby bibs and hats and toddler t-shirts proudly declare 'I'm a little angel!'
- I have items of all descriptions in my house … it's amazing how many of them are covered with or decorated with angels. If you took a quick walk around my house you would find dishes with angels sitting on the side, an angel clock, an angel sitting on a mirror, angels decorating candles and candlesticks, angels on oil-burners, angel rainbow crystals in my windows, angel figurines, and a plate and a plant pot decorated with copies of paintings of angels from the Sistine Chapel. If you look a little closer you will discover angels hiding around the garden, angels on pictures, angel cards, angel books and angel music CDs. The list is endless (you'll find pictures on my website).
- Buying products can be expensive, but many of the items I was given as gifts. You can build your collection up over time, or even make some items of your own. Which brings me nicely to point number six!
- Have you ever had a go at glass-painting, drawing or painting angels or writing angel poetry? Among the gifts

people have given me are a knitted angel and an angel draught-excluder! I own cats, and someone once sent me a cat toy shaped like an angel (I'm serious! It was filled with cat-nip and the cats just loved it). I bet you can think of many more ideas: lampshades, cushions and even blanket throws have angels on them now – why not make your own? If you can't draw you can purchase angel stencils ... I've decorated a box with them, used glass paints to paint a glass candle-holder, used ceramic paints to decorate a pencil pot, and created a silk cushion cover decorated with angel images. If I can do it then so can you. Are you feeling inspired yet?

- Why not create a space in your home where you display your angels? Some people call this an 'angel altar'. You can have a lot of fun with arranging this. First find a pretty cloth to display things on. A sparkly scarf, small tablecloth or just a scrap of pretty material will work just fine. Add an angel figurine or two, a candle in a pretty holder, some fresh flowers, perhaps a crystal or two, and then include a box or bowl to place any angel feathers you find. You can also use this area to store your angel books, special family photographs, shells or maybe angel divination cards.

- Connecting to the angels is just a state of mind. Your angels are always with you ... the trick is to become more aware of their subtle signs. Reading about the angels (like you're doing with this book) can certainly make you more aware. Hundreds of you write and tell me about the experiences you have whilst you are reading my books or immediately afterwards ... they can't all be coincidences! Reading about angels puts you in the 'zone'! You can build up your collection over time. Ask for angel books as gifts, or check out book sales, supermarkets, charity shops and libraries. You can often get bargains on the internet (check you aren't overpaying for postage and packaging, though). Authors such as myself will usually sell personally signed copies (if you prefer this), and many of my fans share their books amongst family and friends (make sure you put your name inside and keep a record of who has borrowed your book so it eventually finds its way back home (be warned – they often don't!).

- Spreading a little angel happiness can be as simple as sending a letter on angel-decorated writing paper. You can easily add an angel icon to your notes if you use a computer, or buy sheets of angel stickers at craft shops and use them to decorate your envelopes. I own several gold angel 'stampers' and a gold stamp pad. I use these to decorate all my post, the envelopes in particular, and people seem to love this. Look for angel confetti (from card shops) and include some silver or gold cherubs in every greetings card (I like to add a warning on the envelope so the glittery pieces don't end up in someone's dinner!). Look for angel birthday and Christmas cards. Buy them when you see them (I wait until they are reduced after Christmas, as I use so many). Keep a stock in ready for any occasion. Scour gift shops, supermarkets and garden centres for angel figurines, which are often reduced after Christmas. The large fabric 'tree topper' angels are expensive to buy, but in the January sales you can often buy them for half price or cheaper. Angel tree decorations look wonderful hanging from a small branch attached to your conservatory ceiling, or you can use the decorations to make an angel mobile. I have angels sitting on the edge of many of my plants or 'tacked' to the edge of shelves (use the putty-type 'tac' to attach small figurines to shelves, especially if you have cats like I have).

- Don't forget your outside space! I have a collection of scented flowers in pots surrounding my front door. Of course these are encircled by angel plant sticks, outdoor fairy lights, an angel wind-chime and a little statue of an angel reading a book! I've chosen scented plants because they are especially connected to the angels. Many people smell beautiful flowers when they experience angel contact, so I've added lavender, roses, pinks and scented geraniums to my collection. I'm sure you will have your own favourites. Because I have a covered porch I'm lucky enough to have room for a couple of basket chairs, one each side of the front door. It's fairly private and in the warm weather is a delightful place to sit and read … angel books, of course! Each chair has its own cushion … decorated with a fairy (Nature's angels).

- Something I've suggested before, but is always worth repeating, is to create an angel journal. This is the perfect place to write about your angel experiences … or favourites that you've read about. You can buy a pretty notebook or create something from scratch. Maybe use hand-pressed paper or sparkly card to make the cover. Perhaps you could paint something or create a decoupage cover (lots of little cut-out images stuck down to create one larger image). You might prefer to buy something pretty especially for the purpose. Try creating some angel-inspired writing: ask the angels to send you a message (some people call this *channelling*) or help you to write beautiful poetry. When you're happy with the finished piece, use beautiful writing or maybe type up and print off your work on the computer and stick it into your book. Victorian ladies loved keeping a nature journal which, accomplished as they were, they would illustrate with drawings or watercolour paintings. You could create something equally gorgeous but using all the modern craft tools we have available. Add love to your angel journal and illustrate it with stickers, photographs and even angel feathers.

- Talking of nature … angels love outdoor spaces. The higher energy of the natural realms makes it easier for them to draw near to us. Water is an especially powerful medium, so if you can take regular breaks by the sea or by a river, stream or lake you are in the perfect place to achieve angel contact. If this is difficult for you, try adding a water feature to your outdoor space. If you don't have a garden or yard, an indoor water feature (a fountain in a bowl) is the perfect solution. I have one next to my desk in my office. The sound of the waterfall is always relaxing. I've placed mine on a large terracotta plant dish (from my local garden centre) to stop it splashing on the floor, and filled it with shells and crystals … beautiful and relaxing. Propped on the side of the water well is … you've guessed it, another angel!

TOO MANY ANGELS?

You can never have too many angels in your life (although my husband might disagree with that!) … I'm talking about both the ones you've bought or created as well as the feathered kind. Your 'intent' is so important. The energy you put out is the energy you receive back again … it works like a mirror and you make your own reflection of life.

Loving thoughts and deeds create a loving life. As you can see, I live and breathe angels in my life … they are everything to me. Paranormal phenomena happen every day. Things which some might find frightening (because they really make you think) do not scare me at all. If I ask for a sign, I get one. If I ask for help, it arrives. If I need something in my life, it appears for me … and you can have this, too.

Plug yourself into the angel energy. Live and breathe the angels in your life and make sure you are always open to their guidance … but most of important of all, when the angels draw close and you feel their help, remember to say, 'Thank you, angels.'

ASK, ASK, ASK

Your angels can help you in so many different situations, but you do have to keep giving them permission. Need help starting the car, getting a new job or just cleaning the windows? Angels might alert a neighbour, arrange for you to bump into someone needing your skills or provide you with a new ladder. Their help can arrive in many ingenious ways.

Gifts from Heaven?

'My brother passed away suddenly on 28th November 2008; he was just 41 years old … I have been having a very hard time dealing with his death. I know that there is a song called "Pennies from Heaven", but on three separate occasions, dimes have appeared out of nowhere for me.

'The first time my mother-in-law and I were at my son's hockey game and we were in the warm seating area waiting for his game to start. All of a sudden a dime fell out of the sky in front of her. Now, her left hand was holding her gloves and her right hand was holding her bottle of water … and one of my hands was holding a cup of coffee and the other was in my pocket. My husband was beside me holding my daughter and no one else was around … where did this dime come from?

'The second time this occurred, I was doing my washing. I'd taken the towels out of the washer to put into my dryer and, just as I did that, another dime appeared. Now, the dime wasn't there when I'd taken the previous load out and I couldn't figure where it might have come from.

'The third time was when I was cleaning my bedroom and I had some clothes on the floor folded in a pile. I started sorting through the clothes and found yet another dime. I'm sure my brother is coming through from the other side for me.'
– Denise, Canada

Pennies, crystals and small pieces of jewellery are often moved about or made to appear or disappear. I'd love to receive sums of cash being deposited in and around my home, but not so sure I would want an angel 'spiriting away' a piece of jewellery!

One of the most common 'gifts' is feathers.

Three Feathers in One Day

'My eldest daughter started senior school and my little boy had just joined the reception class. As you might guess, I was feeling a little lost and missing my late father. I wanted to share the changes in my life that he is no longer around to see. I longed for him to bring me a sign that he is still around me and my children.

'My little boy came out of school a little upset because another boy had stolen his feather. I asked him what he meant and he said that a big white feather had floated down into the playground and my son had played with it for a while before it was taken by another child. I realized that if the feather hadn't been taken I might never have realized he'd even found one.

'We picked up my middle daughter from the juniors and then went to collect my eldest daughter from seniors. While we were waiting, my middle daughter said, 'Mummy, did you see that white feather?' I hadn't, but she was so pleased and immediately mentioned Grandad because she felt it was a sign from him.

'We chatted about the feathers in the car on the way home, but my eldest became upset because she felt she hadn't had her own feather sign. Yet as we stopped at the lights, a white feather came floating down in front of the car, almost as though it was in slow motion.

'She was thrilled and so was I. I could not believe that three of my children had each seen a feather in three different places and all on the same day!'

– Suzanne, England

What is your angel gift or sign? These connections are very personal. If your late father was a big car fan, then maybe your sign from him would be related to the cars he loved in life. If Great-grandma always baked chocolate cake, then her sign to you might be related to her speciality dish. Signs are individual and personal – often unique to a person or family. What are your family signs?

ASKING FOR A SIGN

If you're hoping for a sign from a passed-over loved one, you don't always have to visit a psychic medium to get your message. As well as visiting in dreams, our loved ones bring all sorts of signs and signals from the other side of life.

Make a note of anyone you would particularly like to hear from. What signs do you associate with them? Ask for your sign … and then be prepared to see a series of 'coincidences'. One sign is not normally enough and you are likely to pick up on several things over the course of a couple of days or so:

- You hear your special word or phrase on the radio (especially if you just happen to walk into a shop and your song is playing in the background).
- A presenter uses your particular word … especially if you've just turned on the television … or someone else has!
- An article in a magazine stands out to you – especially if you pick the magazine up unconsciously and randomly flick to the page.
- Someone brings you a gift related to your sign.
- The topic comes up in the book you are reading.
- You spot the letters that form your chosen sign on car number plates or posters.
- People use your sign-word in a sentence unexpectedly (assuming you haven't talked to them in advance about your sign). Angels and those on the other side will often influence people to bring a sign to you.

CELEBRITIES WHO BELIEVE

In my book *Angels Watching Over Me* I wrote a whole section on celebrities and even royals who believe in angels or an afterlife.

Belief in a higher power is right back where it should be, as part of everyone's normal everyday life.

I've interviewed many famous people who believe in angels or even 'work' with their guardian angels on a daily basis. I'm glad they don't mind talking about their experiences in public … it makes my life a lot easier!

Even Hollywood 'A-listers' are among this group; people like actor Denzel Washington, who says he had an angel encounter when he was a small boy. He says the figure looked a little like his sister at first glance, but the vision had wings. No sooner had he spied the angel than it disappeared, and afterwards when he told his mother what he had seen she immediately reassured him that the being must have been his guardian angel.

… AND CELEBRITY 'ANGELS'

The famous also feature in the afterlife visitation experience … even when the person seeing the vision never knew the celebrity in life, apparently. Elvis Presley is one whom people regularly see at the pearly gates (after the usual angels, guides and deceased relatives, of course)! This information comes from those who've had near-death experiences (NDE) … and have come back to life again to share their stories.

Princess Diana and the late 'animal man' Steve Irwin are regularly seen by fans around the world who've mourned their passing (lots of whom also write to me!). Death does not seem to prevent these loving souls from reaching out to those who care about them on this side of life. These famous souls are usually seen in dream-visitation experiences – real visits from these souls.

ANGEL MEDITATION

Your angels are always trying to reach out to you, even if you're not aware of it. Our verbal language is so important to us that we do tend to switch off the other senses. Yet the blind have super-acute senses. Those whose visual abilities are diminished or missing learn to tune in to their other senses. Would a person who is visually impaired be more likely to sense an angel? Probably!

Do you want to learn to tune in to your own guardian angel's messages? First you have to tune out everything else around you. If you're expecting your angel to talk to you in a normal 'human' voice, then you might be lucky but they don't usually communicate with us in this way. Last night I was awoken by someone calling my name … but I know the voice was inside my head. I wish it happened more often, as I love this sort of communication.

'Real voice' messages are usually reserved for emergencies – and even then it's only a word or three!

Angel contact is more likely to be:

- a feeling or sense of something
- a 'realization' or 'inspirational' thought – that moment when you go 'I know what to do now!' (but you don't know where the idea came from)
- a physical touch (a hand in your hand … or a hand on your shoulder)
- flickering lights (or some people see balls of light … or orbs)
- an outline or shape which glows (mothers see the outline of an angel watching over their babies in their cribs, for example)

- you notice a big change ... or 'coincidence' ... that happens right after you shout 'help'
- most common, you feel that you're at the end of the line, there is no one left to turn to and you see no way out of your predicament, yet assistance arrives and often in the most bizarre way possible
- music (usually described as choir-like or made up of beautiful harmonies) or a couple of words (speaking is not natural to angels as their communication is by telepathic thought ... whole ideas transmitted at once).

MUSIC

Nai heard angel music. She told me,

'This morning I woke to the lovely sound of music being played softly in my left ear. The music was something I have never heard before, but I did ask the angels if this was their own music, and they said yes.
I did feel a lot more relaxed and happier after hearing the music (I have been under a lot of pressure of late).'

Hearing angel music is not so common. I was lucky enough to hear the sound of a beautiful choir following a request to the angels to help my sick daughter. I understand why people believe that angels sit around on clouds all day playing harps! No doubt this idea came about as a result of earlier folk who were lucky enough to pick up on the beautiful harmonies from the heavenly realms ... said to be the angels praying to God.

Music seems to be the angels' natural way of communicating ... yet many people are disappointed when the angels don't speak to them! Words of comfort usually come in the form of the voice of a spiritual guide (perhaps acting on the request of the angels) or in the voice of a deceased loved one.

For a brief moment in time, when our lives are in danger or we are in distress, a deceased loved one may whisper words of comfort or advice. I have hundreds of stories like this in my many books.

WORDS

Jean heard several words, but she was never sure if the words came telepathically or if she actually heard the words with her physical ears. She told me,

'My mother was sick and I asked my angels to help me to cope with what was to come. I was sitting at home when I heard a voice say that the doctors would find something on my mother's lung. Two days later we were told that she had to get tests done because they'd found something on her lung. I then asked the angels what was wrong with her; again I heard a voice, this time it said my mother had cancer. So far we have not been told this news but I feel I have been warned.'

Many would ask, is this real? How do I know that I didn't 'make this up'?

Practice is the only way, and in time you do learn the difference between your thoughts and the angels'. Keep accurate notes so that you can always follow up with these thoughts and feelings. Messages from your angels are always loving and kind … even when giving bad news. You won't hear your angels chastising you or being sarcastic. It simply doesn't work that way.

What one person calls a bad experience, another calls a challenge or an opportunity to learn and grow. Bigger questions like, 'Why did my son have to die?' simply don't have a single, straightforward answer that would satisfy anyone. One thing I have learned over the years is that when loved ones visit from the 'other side of life', appearing during our sleeping hours, it's a question that many are asked: 'Why did you die?'

After my own father passed away he appeared in several dreams to different members of the family to explain why he had died when he did. Dad let us know that he had had a choice of several dates on which to pass over. He chose the earliest date because his physical body was at the healthiest it would be (and he was already very sick). He showed us that if he had lived longer, both he and, as a result, the rest of his family would have suffered dreadfully in many different ways (stress, worry, inconvenience).

Maybe on some level we all choose in advance, for reasons of our own … I'm sure one day we will find out why. All I can tell you is the most common answer to this question when a soul this side of life asks a relative why they died, is … 'It was my time.'

PROBLEM SOLVING

Angels are great at coming up with solutions you've never even dreamed about – ask for help, and let them do their job. However, if you don't want to save your angel contact only for emergencies, then there are techniques you can learn.

Meditation can help to bring the angels closer. By relaxing you raise your spiritual 'vibration' and the more you meditate the higher your vibration (the more relaxed you are). People experience angel contact (particularly the more dramatic encounters) when their body is in an altered state of consciousness. The most common times for an angel experience are:

- during 'bodily sleep' (the mind is usually aware and 'lucid' during angel or spirit visitation)
- when the body is unconscious – during an operation, for example
- after fainting – your own spirit might momentarily leave your body and it's possible to see your physical body lying beneath you as you drift onwards and upwards
- during times of trauma and deep stress
- in moments of great fear (when your whole body is on high alert)
- when day-dreaming ... or performing automatic tasks (we say the body is on 'auto-pilot' ... the sort of thing that happens when an experienced driver is driving a familiar route)
- during boring tasks the body is also more likely to receive afterlife contact (angels or deceased loved ones) as the mind also wanders ... we call it day-dreaming; examples are when you're doing the ironing, washing-up and so on
- during normal sleep
- when the body is on the edge of sleep – both just before sleeping or just before awakening. This is when I get most of my own visitation encounters
- when the body is exhausted but the mind is overactive and stimulated. This creates a sort of separation in the body/ mind when the normal rules no longer apply. Your body may fall into an exhausted sleep, and indeed you may even hear yourself snore, but your mind has not switched off and remains aware
- in times of deep relaxation: on holiday, sitting in a hot tub, walking along a river bank and so on.

Once you achieve a floating feeling you are more receptive to your angel's messages to you. Naturally it makes sense then to induce this 'floating feeling' in a completely safe 'relaxation' state. Meet the angels … on purpose!

HOW TO MEDITATE WITH YOUR ANGELS

1. First of all, create a safe place so that you can relax. That might mean you meditate in your bedroom, or at least in a room with a door so you can shut out the world and not be disturbed.

2. Take the phone off the hook, take the baby to the babysitter's and the dog to the neighbours (or get a family member to take the dog for a lovely long walk!).

3. You might want to keep a soft blanket handy or wear socks so you don't get cold, and make sure you dress in loose clothing so you can be as relaxed as possible.

4. Select some gentle music (many new age shops sell 'angel music' specifically for the purpose of meditating or relaxation; this is a perfect choice). Wearing headphones helps to block out the sound of the world around you.

5. You might wish to light a candle, which helps to create a sacred space (I suggest a tea light in a glass jar or glass candle-holder standing on a tray, in a safe place, well out of your way).

6. Find a comfortable place to sit … preferably in an upright chair … or sit cross-legged on the floor if you are a little more agile. You can lie down and meditate, but you may fall asleep.

Many people find it easier to use a guided meditation (or visualization 'journey' – where a voice talks you through a visualized walk to a special place). This can be easier when you are first learning to meditate. A pre-meditation relaxation exercise is normally built in to these. Many shops sell them and I have created several of my own ('Meet your Guardian Angel', 'Healing with Your Guardian Angel' ... for more information visit: www. AngelLady.co.uk).

Read through the following exercise a few times and memorize it. Don't worry if you forget anything, the experience will become personal to you and each time you 'visit' your meditation space (your journey) you will remember more and more. Are you ready?

Relaxation

First you need to relax. (If you're following a recording then you will probably be able to skip this stage and just listen to the instructions on your recording. This exercise assumes you are using music only for your meditation – YOU create the rest of the visualization by using the text below.)

The idea is that you relax each part of the body in turn. Start with your toes ... relax ... then the soles of your feet ... relax ... now your heels ... relax ... now concentrate on your ankles ... relax (and so on). Start at the bottom of your body and work your way to the top.

I won't bore you by listing out each limb, but just imagine each section in turn and tell yourself to relax (you might wish to flex the body part and then relax it ... some people find this easier). If you prefer you can start at the top and work your way down.

The Journey

Imagine yourself walking along a path. You find a gate and open it, walk through ... closing the gate behind you (this helps you to feel safe during your visualization – if this is your first time you may even want to 'lock' your gate behind you, hanging the key on a soft and pretty 'ribbon' around your neck). Take in all the details as you walk along your path: the birds are singing, there is bouncy grass beneath your feet. 'Look' at the variety of plant life around you, smell the scent and enjoy the colours of the flowers.

Look ahead and see a clearing with a bench ... stroll towards this and sit down, noticing as you do so the wonderful view ahead. What is your view? Do you see mountains, lakes, a river, or perhaps the sea? The choice is yours. Create whatever pleases you most.

While you are relaxing in this wonderful place, you become aware of your guardian angel's presence. Your angel brings unconditional love, and you sense and feel this. Take a moment to savour this feeling. Enjoy it. Let it wash over you ... then draw the love into your body. Feel it – really sense the love that the angel sends your way.

Now you see your angel in front of you. What does he or she look like: a ball of light? A glowing figure? A human-looking figure with wings? Take in the colour of your angel's skin, the colour of his or her eyes ... what is your angel wearing? How does he or she feel? Enjoy the experience and remember it so that you can recall this moment later.

You can hug your angel if it feels right or perhaps you sit together and hold hands – whatever is comfortable at this moment. This is your opportunity to ask your guardian angel anything you want to. Talk for as long as you like.

Talking to Your Angel

Things you might like to ask or request:

1. Ask for guidance and direction for an ongoing problem (money, weight, etc.).
2. Ask your angel's name.
3. Request protection for yourself or a loved one.
4. Call upon your angels to assist others in need.
5. Your angels might be able to help you get a new job, or train for a new career.
6. Ask for an 'upgrade' in specific skills (extra courage or more confidence, for example).
7. Your angels could certainly help you to find new friends.
8. How about asking your angels if you can help them?

Some folk are so overwhelmed when they come face to face with their guardian angel that they immediately forget what they wanted to ask. I'm sure you'll find it helpful to create a list first of all. After you've completed your meditation session, write down a few notes so you don't forget (your 'few notes' may well stretch to several pages).

Receiving Messages

Another idea is to ask your guardian angel for a message or a symbolic gift. Your role is just to listen or watch the proceedings and then, as before, record your experience. You may find that you remember more and more or recall more and more meanings in the days that follow your meditation experience. Once you're 'plugged in' to angel guidance, I'm sure the messages will just continue to flow.

Create Your Own Meditation Experiences

How good is your imagination? If you are a creative person you'll enjoy creating your own meditation journeys. Take a notebook and pen ... or a sit at a computer if you're technically minded. Write your own journeys to commune with your guardian angels. Here are a few suggestions:

- Meet on the sea shore.
- Fly up to greet your angels by travelling in a balloon.
- Float together in a bubble.
- Get together in a crystal or marble building.
- Become a ball of light and meet your angels in their natural state ... energy.
- 'Try on' an animal body (your spirit animal) – become a tiger or a stag ... or ask your angel to appear in this way.
- Journey in your mind to a spiritual location on Earth.
- Project your spirit to a planet far away and meet your angels and guides there.

The list is endless and only limited by your ability to perceive. Write down your journey first of all and then try it out for real. If you're really adventurous you could try 'free-flow' meditation journeys: close your eyes and go wherever you feel drawn! You'll be perfectly safe as your angel will be at your side. Remember, you can end the meditation at any time simply by opening your eyes. You are in charge at all times.

Surround yourself with your angel's love as you do this, and remember that the worst that can happen is that you fall asleep!

Record Your Experiences

Always make a note of your experiences. This is a useful way of watching your progress. Remember to describe how you feel as well as what you've seen and heard. Make notes of:

1. The date and time of your experience
2. The location (where were you – sitting in your conservatory? Lying on the bed?)
3. What sort of journey did you take? Where did you go? Were there variations on previous experiences?
4. Did you meet your angel? What did you observe about him/ her?
5. What messages did your angel give you?
6. What symbols were you shown?
7. What did you see (did any particular colours stand out)?
8. Did you encounter anyone else during your journeying (a spirit guide, a deceased relative or an animal, for example)?

Guided meditations or inspirational journeying is a wonderful way not only to meet your angel but to collect inspiration for every one of life's challenges. Tune out your physical world and go and visit your inner world today – you've nothing to lose.

ANGELS OR HUMANS?

Let's have one last look at angelic humans before we leave this chapter. Are the mysterious angels that some people see true angels, or angelic humans? Many times when a person appears at the scene of an accident they help and then mysteriously disappear. Now, it's possible that your helper is just shy and doesn't want praise, but is it really likely that someone would help you and then disappear?

Here is a story that reflects this phenomenon. Is this a human angel or a celestial angel?

'Mini' Angel

'In the 1970s, when my son was still at primary school, I collected him at the school gate and told him that I wanted to pop to the shops in the next village to buy a cake tin so that we could bake a cake together when we got home.

'It was only a five-minute journey to the shops and, although there was a light dusting of snow on the ground, there seemed nothing to worry about. Just after we started off the snow suddenly came down like a blizzard. It was a winding country lane and suddenly I lost control of the car and skidded into a ditch. The car landed with one side down in the ditch. I was terrified.

'My son banged his head on the window and I was shaken but unscathed. When I tried to open the door on my side to get us out of the car I wasn't strong enough to push it open. I tried several times and then started to panic a bit. It was a quiet country lane and no one in their right mind would be out on it in those conditions.

'Then I noticed a little Mini car came around the bend, and stopped. A very tall lady got out of the car (I was amazed she could fit in her car!). She strode over to us and opened the door very easily. I don't really remember getting in her little car or much about the journey home, but I do remember thanking her and saying it was really kind of her and that I hoped she wasn't going out of her way … a strange thing to say considering I'd just been in an accident! She said that it wasn't a problem.

'The lady took us straight home, although I can't even remember whether I ever told her where we lived! As I walked down the drive to our door, I turned to wave my thanks again but the car had completely disappeared. It would have taken someone quite a while to turn a car around in our lane with all the snow that had fallen, and some shunting backwards and forwards, so I have no idea how she managed it in such a speedy time.

'I didn't think about guardian angels then, but now I look back I do think that this lady was an angel sent to help us. Since then, many years forward I have become extremely interested in guardian angels and the afterlife, and understand now that I had been getting signs for some time but didn't realize.'
– Glenda, England

Earth Angels

All around the world you hear of people performing heroic acts of kindness … people who act as angels on Earth. I decided to do a quick search on the internet for some recent stories that made the news.

Rosalia DeSantis, a 58-year-old woman, was rescued from almost certain death after she fainted and fell 1.5 metres onto train tracks below her. Two men jumped down and rescued her with just seconds to spare.

Then there was 72-year-old Jane Cropper, who passed out after hitting a tree in her truck. No sooner had the truck come to a halt than it immediately burst into flames. Luckily for Jane, three men she describes as her 'guardian angels' lifted her free. The three men just happened to be passing the scene at the time and, strangely, one of the men had already stopped once on his journey … to help another woman change a flat tyre!

WHO BELIEVES?

According to a report by Baylor University's Institute for Studies of Religion, over half of all adults in the USA believe in guardian angels. The survey polled Americans of all religious backgrounds, including those with no religion. More women than men believe in these supernatural messengers. Many of those polled felt they'd had angelic intervention at least once in their lives.

Common to these experiences is an 'angel' who helps them out in extreme circumstances and then, once they are safe, just disappears. It's likely that at least some of these encounters are with human 'angels' … but then in most cases we'll probably never really know for sure.

An informal study of Britons carried out by retailer ChoicesUK identified that 68 per cent believed that ghosts and spirits exist … maybe as a result of the current fad for 'ghost-hunting' as a pastime! I couldn't find a poll for Britons relating to angels, but I wouldn't be surprised if the results were fairly similar.

Angels appear in many guises; I think we often don't realize until afterwards that we might, just might, have encountered one. If you come across someone who's particularly tall with blond or white hair and piercing blue eyes, take a second look – because you never know! (Then, of course, drop me a line and tell me all about it!)

9

Wisdom and Feathers

'I wear a coat of angel's breath and warm myself with His love.'
– Emme Woodhull-Bäche

WHAT IS AN ANGEL?

Children adore angels. Many learn about them during the school nativity play, but often children know about angels before adults explain who and what they are. I asked parents on my Facebook page to ask their own little ones the question, 'What is an angel?' Here are their fun (and touching) replies.

- Daniel (9) – 'They are who you live with when you're dead and before mummy gets us.'
- Alex (5) – 'It has wings … and some carry candles.'
- Callum (9) – 'It's the person that keeps dropping white feathers for Paul, Mummy's boyfriend!'
- Charlie (6) – 'An angel is what my nanny is now.'
- Nathaniel (6) – 'It's a thing with wings!'
- Declan (12) – 'They're light, they can fly and they can't die.'

- Aimee (7) – 'An angel is made out of light.'
- Connal (5) – 'When they are on the ground they have wings and when they are up in the sky they are balls.'
- Madison (3) – 'They are up with God, they look white and some are good, and some are bad, and some make us better; and when they are in an egg they can't fly!'
- Ben (2) – 'It's what you become when you die!'
- Amber (11) – 'An angel takes care of you when you're feeling sad so you never feel alone …'

From Mums

'When Gabriella was about six, she was asked to paint a picture of her idea of heaven. Well, she painted the whole page blue. She was upset when she came home, as she'd been told off for not doing it "properly". When I asked her about it, she said, "Heaven makes me feel all soft, beautiful and blue." The teacher apologized and said she'd learned something very precious that day!'

'My seven-year-old said an angel is someone who looks after you and is in heaven, and my 10-year-old says it's a person with wings who loves you. My 13-year-old says an angel guides you through life and helps you make the right decisions. Lauren (my seven-year-old) also just told me they are 'God's messengers' – apparently they were told that at school.'

- Jordan (9) – 'They are flying people with rings over their heads that give you messages.'
- Milo (12) – 'An angel is something that helps you when you're in trouble and looks over you and makes you feel all warm like when I was ill and had a feather on my bed and

my mum said I might have been visited by an angel, and that made me smile.'

- Travis (6) – 'Angels are good people that died and went to heaven, and they look after us all and send and grant messages.'
- Katie (11) – 'An angel is like a diamond, you can't just find them, you have to search for them truthfully, and when you find them they are like a treasure to you.'
- Oliver (11) – 'It depends whether it's a guardian angel or the Christmas ones! An angel is someone that looks after you to ensure that you are OK in the day, and to guide you through the day.'
- Milly (10) – 'It's kind of a fairy that lives in heaven and will help you when you ask.'
- Lucy (6) – 'An angel is … an angel.'
- Chelsea-Jayne (13) – 'An angel is someone who helps you when you are feeling sad and looking for guidance.'
- Emma (9) – 'An angel wears white clothes with fluffy wings and gives you advice and works for God.'
- Fraser (3) – 'Angels are like my sister' (she is 15, and his Mum begs to differ!).

From Mums

'My son Kevin, who is five, came to my room to crawl into bed with me late one night. He said when he came into my room it was very dark, but he saw a lady in a chair alongside my bed knitting and watching me as I slept. He said she was an angel.'

'Afternoon, Jacky. After seeing your status the other day [on Facebook] asking about what children think about angels, I asked my five-year-old daughter Lisa. As I was sat reading my angel book at the time, she looked at the picture on the cover and said, "Angels are fairies with fluffier wings." I asked her what an angel's job is and she said, "They help people up to the sky and saving children that can't fly when they are asleep."'

'I asked my neighbour's four-year-old son and he said that he was an angel when Grandma came over.'

- **Kial (5) – 'When you're dead you turn into an angel.'**
- **Robert (7) – 'They've got feathers as wings.'**
- **Charlotte (9) – 'Peace, love and God.'**
- **Mia-Isabella (10) – 'Care, belief, and happiness.'**
- **Kyle (9) – 'Jesus, cross, families and Mum.'**

So there you go – if you ever want any information about angels, ask a child, because they know everything there is to know about angels!

FEATHERS
White feathers have become known as the 'calling card' of a visiting angel. It's the one sign that people seem to receive when they ask for proof that an angel is around them or when they ask the angels to draw near. The angels often respond by bringing a feather 'gift'.

We've already seen angel stories in this book that include feathers. Many of the stories people send me include white feathers. These can be anything from the tiny white 'baby bird' feathers to beautiful curled, perfectly white swan's feathers. Other stories involve multi-coloured feathers … which may or may not have different meanings (some believe yes and others think no).

These little symbols are a perfect sign of comfort. Once found they can be carried around in your purse or pocket, or given to someone in need. Some collect their angel feathers and gather them together in a special box or jar ... whatever feels comfortable for you.

People often ask me if those who believe in angels are more likely to see an angel sign. I think the question should be, do those who open their hearts to an angel presence have more experiences? Human souls follow the universal law of free will. We make our own choices in life and angels help us when we tell them that they may intercede. Invite your angels to take part in your life. Literally give them permission to intervene, and they will.

By reading and talking about angels we set up a vibration of energy around us which is particularly attractive (in the magnetic sense) to the angels. It's like we send out a torch beam which says, 'Hey ... I'm here.' Keep your energy beam bright and light. Make sure that all thoughts you send out are loving ones (both to the higher realms and to human souls in and around your life) ... work extra hard to think good thoughts about people you don't currently like!

Look out for feathers on the ground, especially those indoors or in unusual locations. Feathers can fall from the sky or fly past you ... I've caught them in mid-air after asking for a sign!

Feathers have long been associated with spirituality. They are a traditional shamanic tool. The ancient shaman (which translates as 'The One Who Knows') or healer, would use feathers in rituals which cleansed the aura (energy field) or chakras (energy centres of the body). The feather symbolically makes the communication or energy 'fly' to wherever it is needed.

Here is a fun feather story.

Bread Feather

'After reading in one of your books about white feathers as a sign of an angel's presence, I decided one Thursday evening in August that I would love to receive a white feather from my angels, so I asked them if they would kindly send me one.

'The next day I went into our spare bedroom. I was looking under the bed, the chair and even the table for the carrier bag in which I had put my spare work uniform. Unable to find the bag, I gave up looking. The next day (Saturday) I went into the same bedroom, sat on the bed and just happened to look down by the chair (where I'd been the day before on my hands and knees looking for the carrier bag). I saw something white on the carpet, so I bent down and picked it up. I was shocked to find a white feather because I knew there hadn't been one there the day before. Even more strange, right next to it was a baby white feather!

'I was absolutely delighted and really impressed at the speed with which my angels had answered my request. I put my two white feathers in a little container and kept it on my bedside table, so I would have a constant physical reminder of my beautiful angel's presence.

'Later I thought how fabulous it would be if I could have one more feather, so that I could keep one container upstairs and one downstairs. Once again I asked my angels if they would oblige me with one more feather.

'A few days later I arrived home from work and my mum asked me to go into the kitchen and slice the French baguette that she had bought that day. I opened the carrier bag and took out one half of the baguette (my mum had broken it into two pieces so it would fit in the bag). I was stood with a knife in my other hand ready to start slicing when I noticed something fluffy sticking to the bread. I turned the bread to face me, and to my absolute joy and delight there was a gorgeous white feather staring at me – it was "sitting" in the bread! I asked my mum if she had dropped the bread anywhere or had used an old carrier bag, but everything was new and fresh from the supermarket that day!

'How brilliant! I now know that, not only are my angels listening, but they have a wonderful sense of humour; and I've kept smiling ever since. Now I have my single feather downstairs, and the other two upstairs! Both lots of feathers are a beautiful and constant reminder of the angels' loving presence.

'Thank you, Jacky, for writing about white feathers in your books, and thank you to my loving angels for being in my life!'
– Bina, England

Do you have a little pot that you could use to collect angel feathers? Place a little jar or trinket box (with a lid) by your own bed ready. I'm sure you'll soon have feathers to fill it.

The sign of a simple white feather can bring people the most amazing comfort that 'everything will be OK'. After the loss of a loved one we need these signs that heaven has things 'under control'.

Annabelle and her family were devastated after her baby niece was stillborn but the little feather signs gave them a symbol that she was OK … in another dimension.

Born Asleep

'Three days after my niece was born "sleeping", my partner was working on my car because it had broken down. I was an emotional wreck – we were all devastated about this unexpected and very sad news – and I was just gazing out of the window watching him. All of a sudden about five or six feathers fell to the ground in front of him – they just fell from the sky. Straight away I read this as a sign that my niece was at peace, and it really helped me.

'A couple of weeks later my mum and my sister-in-law's mum both found single white feathers on different days. They both kept the feathers for my sister-in-law to see, and when she had both the feathers together, the strange thing was that they were both the same size and shape, and both pure white. It has really helped us all.'

– Annabelle, England

Tracy's story is similar in that she needed just a little comfort. Is there anybody there to give you a heavenly hug? Tracy thinks so:

Feather-Hug

'Last Tuesday I was ironing my work uniform and had been feeling really low and tearful. When I turned the iron off, right there next to the hob was a small white feather. I know it hadn't been there before, and when I picked it up I felt really peaceful.'

Start looking out for your own feathers!

10

I Can See Angels

*'Make yourself familiar with the angels, and behold them
frequently in spirit; for without being seen, they are present with
you.'* – **Francis de Sales**

SEE ANGELS, FEEL THEM, SENSE THEM ...

Angels are beautiful creatures of light. They are described in many
wonderful ways (as by our child-experts in the previous chapter).

In the Bible (Dan. 10:5-6), it says, ' ... His body was like the
beryl, and his face as the appearance of lightning, and his eyes as
lamps of fire, and his arms and his feet like in colour to polished
brass ...' Bright and beautiful indeed!'

Sometimes we see angels, sometimes we feel them ... others
sense them, but always they are with us in times of stress, danger
and loneliness. Angels draw close when we are grieving and hold
our hands when we are frightened. The majestic and powerful
energy of God's divine messengers is always available should we
need it. Close your eyes ... can you feel them? Just relax ... try

when you are lying in a sun-chair or soaking in the bath. The more relaxed you are, the more you will feel them.

Open your mind … their realms are different to ours, their fabric of being is made of something the human eyes cannot see in normal circumstances. They do their best to adapt themselves so that we can visualize them, but usually this occurs only during times of danger … or deep relaxed states of mind.

Why is it that we find it so hard to know that they are around us? In our busy world, we do not make space for the angels. Now is the time to change all this. Loosen up … be still in your mind and invite the angels to enter.

God created the angels to help us, and now at this time in our creation we are becoming aware of them once more. God created humankind with freedom of choice, but angels to act as his guardians and protectors for humankind, for the planet, the universe and everything beyond.

Angels were created with several purposes in mind, including worship of God (which they mainly do in song) and following His word (instructions) relating to the Earth, ministering to his children (humanity, the animals, birds and fish – and likely many other species on other planets).

VOICES OF THE ANGELS

Angels are sometimes collectively called a 'choir of angels' due to their beautiful 'singing' vibration. Occasionally people are privileged to hear this magical song as we've already shown. 1 Corinthians 13:1 reads, 'Though I speak with the tongues of men and of angels, and have not charity, I am become as sounding brass, or a tinkling cymbal.' Revelation 5:11 tells us, ' … I beheld, and I heard the voice of many angels round about the throne …'

Some people hear this angelic choir when angels are around to escort the deceased on their journey. This next story is a little different because the music announced the arrival back on Earth of a deceased loved one who had come for a visit.

Looking for Forgiveness

'Several years ago I lost a good friend to suicide. I was in agony over it and all I could think was, "Why couldn't he come and talk to me? Why didn't he reach out to someone … anyone?" I cried myself to sleep many nights just thinking about him and regretting that I was never given the chance to try and help him.

'One night as I lay in bed asleep, I was awakened by music. The only way I can describe the music is by saying it was "angelic". It was the most angelic music I've ever heard. I saw my friend and he was encircled by a very bright light. It was like a ring of light all around him. He looked at me and said, "I came to let you know that I am more at peace now than I ever was when I was alive. Please forgive me." Then he just faded away.

'I think it was a really nice gesture for him to let me know that, but I still have regrets that I couldn't have done anything to stop him taking his own life.'

– A Reader

These angel voices can make themselves heard at any time and in any place, but they do often come into being at night. I wonder if, on this occasion, they appeared for reassurance, too …?

Sweet Voices

'When I was younger, about seven, I spent every night absolutely terrified of the dark. I slept under the covers for many years. One particular night I was hiding as usual and I heard music and heavenly voices. It wasn't like anything I'd heard before, and at seven years old it scared the life out of me.

'It's hard to describe such a beautiful chorus, I only know that it filled the whole room and was so powerful. Imagine the biggest choir you can, with the sweetest voices and you still wouldn't be anywhere near the sound. I got so scared that I started to cry and told the voices to go away. Immediately the music stopped and I fell asleep. In the morning I told mum what had happened, and I made my brother play his stereo in his bedroom to see if he'd been playing a trick on me, but nothing could replicate the sound. It was only years later that my mum told me that the same thing had happened to her in the same bedroom. In hindsight I wish I hadn't told the voices to go, as I would dearly love to hear that beautiful sound again. I never appreciated it then, which is so sad.'
– Rae, England

HOW MANY ARE THERE?

Angels appear over 250 times in the Bible … they are an important part of God's work. Many other religions, too, mention angels … they are a reality in numerous cultures the world over. Millions have experienced their intervention even if they haven't seen them with their physical eyes.

The word 'angel' means 'messenger', and angels are sometimes referred to as the 'sons of God' or the 'host' of heaven. Their numbers are vast. Hebrews 12:22 suggests, ' … an innumerable company of angels' and Psalms 68:17 reads ' … the chariots of God are twenty thousand, even thousands of angels …' and Revelation 5:11 says, ' … and the number of them was ten thousand times ten thousand, and thousands of thousands ...' More than enough to go round, then.

THEIR PURPOSE

We already know that angels guide and protect us, but in the Bible they have many and varied roles. Looking at how they have helped in the past helps us to understand how they can help us in our own lives.

- They follow orders – and their messages of love come from God (or the 'creator'/source).
- They guard the righteous – the modern-day interpretation shows how they protect us still, as many stories come to me of dramatic angelic rescue.
- They bring answers to our prayers – angels can't solve every problem but these days they help their human charges to work things out for themselves (giving us hints and clues along our life path).
- The angels brought news of the birth of Jesus – I get a lot of letters where mums-to-be learn of their pregnancy through the word of an angel (or deceased loved one) in a dream.
- Angels announced to the disciples that Jesus was resurrected – although we don't hear of many resurrections these days, angels do appear when we pass over to the other side of life and the spirit leaves the physical body. People who have had near-death experiences tell many stories which reflect this.
- The angels give instructions in the Bible – and they still do this. During times of danger it's common to hear a mystery voice suggest driving home a different way, for

example. Sometimes this information arrives as a sort of 'gut instinct'.

- We read that the angels drove the chariots of God – these days I read stories of them taking the wheel of the car ... or flying a plane out of danger!

- They bring encouraging messages – my own deceased father Ron (my own angel) is sneaky in the way he passes on information. I believe that they (our angels and spirit helpers) are restricted in the information that they can give us because situations we live through on Earth help our spirits to grow. Dad will appear in a dream and say things like, 'Well done,' 'Don't worry' or 'I'm proud of you' ... little hints.

- They watch over children – angels still do this, but these days little ones are more likely to see and interact with their angels!

- Angels praise and worship God – this continues, as angelic choir stories show.

- We are told that an angel will announce the end of time – let's hope this never happens! 'The end of times' as we understand it may occur when the Earth is no longer a valid place to live (or is no longer safe). There is much we can do to care for our planet to stave off this time for as long as possible. Some think this is why more angels are gathering at this time ... so, make sure you do your bit to keep the world safe (keep the peace, recycle, and so on)!

BRING THEM INTO YOUR SPACE

In other books of mine I have talked about the different ways in which we can bring angels into our world in a physical way, by bringing objects decorated with angels into our homes. An angel sitting on the edge of your bookcase, or an angel on a picture, will certainly help you to visualize these grandiose beings more easily.

Treat yourself: choose a little angel-something to bring into your space. This could be a postcard, calendar, clock, photo frame … there are plenty of objects to choose from. Scour any gift shop, new age or crystal shop or even the internet to make your purchase. (See Chapter 8 for more on this.)

MORE ON SIGNS AND POSITIVE CHOICES

Angel signs are everywhere and in everyone. You hear a message through the words of a child, a friend, or a stranger whom you meet by chance. You might see a message in a shop poster or traffic sign. My daughter rang to say she'd been turned down for a job she dearly wanted, but as she spoke a white feather flew up and stuck to the window … the angels are with her … and helping her to find a better job (she found one shortly afterwards).

Angels provide us with inspiration and imagination. They work with pure love and light, and our vibrations are at their highest when twinned with their majesty. You can prepare yourself to receive their highest power by keeping your body as your 'temple'. You have been provided with a body to house the spirit. The body has to be maintained by our care, yet many of us neglect the most basic of provisions.

In many parts of the world there are almost too many food choices. We make bad decisions and let our ego-selves make the decisions about what is right for our bodies and minds. It's time to take control over our own minds – you have to overrule the lazy voices (the ones that go, 'I can't be bothered', 'I'm too tired to exercise today', 'I want to eat another doughnut') … can you hear that voice? It's like a young child stamping its feet. 'I want, I want, I want.' At a time in our history when we have more choices than ever before, we should be making clear, healthy choices, yet so many of us eat that third (or fourth) bar of chocolate, open yet another bottle of wine, spend the last of this week's money on a packet of cigarettes or, worst of all, take drugs. The child within is still stamping its feet and having a tantrum. Become the adult that you are. Give yourself only the best that is available to you ... because you're worth it!

Being human means we have freedom of choice ... we can choose, so choose wisely.

Many of our choices are made through habit, but it's just as easy to create a new habit, a healthier habit. If you want to be more spiritually aware or feel and experience your angelic guidance, start making those positive choices today.

Write down your plan ... shop only for healthy foods, diarize your daily walk or swim ... tick off the number of glasses of water you drink during the day. The angels will help you.

WRITE IT DOWN – FOLLOW IT THROUGH

Let's look at some more of your wonderful stories.

Teenager Emma feels her deceased loved ones support her positive choices.

Helping to Make Good Choices

'Until I read your book *An Angel by My Side*, I never believed in the afterlife. After reading about other people's experiences I knew I'd had the exact same things happen to me ... like one day when I was at the park, and another when I was at my gran's house. I always used to see my grandad at the top of the stairs, although at the time I was starting to think I had "lost it".

'As I'm getting older and experiencing more, I think more about my grandad and a cousin I lost, and I know that when I do something I shouldn't, I feel a presence in the room and it goes all cold. I know it's them telling me to stop!

'Most people think I'm crazy when I tell them, but I know I'm not. Sometimes people ask me if I'm scared when they are around, but strangely I'm not. Because the spirits are family and I was close to both of them, I know they'd never hurt me.'
– Emma, England

I did remind Emma about the 'free will' we are all born with. Any spirit, guide or angel is welcome to their opinion, and can warn and suggest things, but in the end we have to make positive and negative choices on our own. Be empowered. YOU decide where and how you want to live your life (even if you do have a little help from loved ones on the other side).

This next story is such a common one, it amazes me how many times people are saved in this way (see, for example, Deb's story back in Chapter 5) … you have to know that for those involved it's simply 'not their time' to die. These stories are so bizarre that they are a little spooky!

Not My Time …

'I was just 15 years old and shopping one Saturday afternoon in Strood, Kent. I was waiting at the pelican crossing for the lights to change so that I could cross the road. It was a cold day and I had my big coat on.

'Eventually the lights changed and the little green man had appeared; the car nearest me had stopped, so I stepped out – but in a split second I had been pulled back by the hood of my coat, so fast that I'm sure I left the ground. Thank goodness, because the car that had been nearest to me had been hit from behind, so hard that it caught my coat as it flew past me. If I hadn't been pulled back at that moment I would have been under that car for sure.

'Panting with shock, I turned to thank the person behind me – but there was no one there. This experience has stayed with me all these years, and the memory is as clear today as it was the day it happened. I decided to ask in my head who it was that had pulled me back, and I heard a voice in my head say, "Angel Miranda". I can only assume that Miranda is my guardian angel.

'I still speak to Angel Miranda today. I have been told that the angels will not intervene in a person's life unless that person has put themselves somewhere where they shouldn't be; it clearly wasn't "my time". I will always be so grateful to Miranda.'
– Debbie, England

Some of these types of 'rescues', where physical activity takes place, do have witnesses. Could you think of another explanation for this 'angel intervention'? Could a man or woman have noticed what was happening and pulled Debbie out of the way of the car … then felt embarrassed, or perhaps were busy, so went about their day, walking very quickly away? Wouldn't you stop to check the person was OK? These experiences are difficult to explain away, aren't they?

This next story describes a wonderful experience of comfort.

Glad Tidings of Comfort and Joy
'One night I was lying in my bed feeling very restless. I was having trouble sleeping because I was broken-hearted over a

boyfriend who'd recently broken up with me. To be honest, I was feeling really sorry for myself.

'As I was lying in bed I heard the tap come on in the kitchen; it sounded like somebody was getting a glass of water. I thought it was strange, because as far as I knew I was the only one home. Moments later my bedroom door opened a little and a small bit of light shone through. I could see it was my Uncle Ron, who had died a couple of years before.

'When I was a child, my Uncle Ron would always come to my room whenever he visited, and sit and talk to me. Anyway, this is why it didn't seem to shock me when he walked over and sat down … it was what he'd always done. I was just a little nervous at first, because, after all, I knew he was dead!

'He told me there was no need for me to be afraid. He told me not to worry about anything and not to be sad. He said everything would be OK, then he disappeared in an instant. Everything was OK and I soon got myself back together.

'I am so thankful for Uncle Ron for coming to visit me that night. He made me feel so much better.'
– **Jane, Canada**

Is being broken-hearted a massive problem in the big scheme of things? Could you compare it to a war, say, or starvation, or someone losing their home? The angels – and our deceased loved ones – don't judge these things, and neither should we. Our problems are our problems, and in this case Jayne certainly needed the comfort a kindly uncle could bring. Love, as always from one dimension to the next, is why he visited.

Jayne's Uncle Ron was sitting on the bed chatting kindly to her, as he'd always done in life. Many spirits do this. Some even make their regular Friday night telephone call … via a dream-visitation, of course!

Dads are always protective of their daughters in life … and this doesn't seem to change in death. Here's Louise's story.

Dad Saved My Life

'In the year 1994, six years after my father passed away, my husband went to bed early as he was feeling unwell. I chose to stay up and watch some TV, and ended up falling asleep on the sofa beneath a lovely warm duvet.

'About 2.45 in the morning I woke to find my deceased father shaking me back and forth. I thought it was a dream, and attempted to go back to sleep, but then I heard a noise coming from my window. At the time I lived in a ground-floor flat, and when I walked over to the window I saw that two men were attempting to get in through the window.

'It was terrifying, but I think they got a bigger fright than I did when they saw me standing there unexpectedly. I don't remember much about it now, or even what I shouted, but I know it scared them away.

'I can't imagine what would have happened if I'd woken up with them in the room, if they'd actually managed to climb in. I really believe that Dad saved my life that day and came back from the other side to watch over me as he would have done when he was alive … thanks, Dad!'

– Louise, Scotland

This next story shows how our pets and loved ones are still around for us … a voice in the graveyard might seem scary at first, but Steven and his family knew it was a loving relative just giving them a few words of reassurance.

My Brother and I Are Psychic

'I first started to realize that I have a strong connection with the afterlife on New Year's Eve 1999. My mother had gone out to a party and I was at home with my younger brother, he's two years younger, and we were watching the TV coverage of the New Year celebrations.

'Although the TV coverage was fun, we were both in a sombre mood. I looked across at my brother and noticed tears were running down his cheeks. I was a bit distressed by this and asked him what was wrong, but he said nothing and didn't realize he'd been crying. More to the point, he said that I too had tears running down my face!

'We both had a feeling of sadness, it was like something was missing. The atmosphere in the house was like static, and everywhere we went in the house it felt as if we were being followed. My brother walked into the front room and then stepped back out, in shock. He'd seen an old man standing by the window, and he got the name "James" from the vision and kept repeating it over and over again. I could feel the man in the room but felt no fear, just awe. Whoever the man was, he had brought the family dog with him.

'Our darling pet had been put down the previous November, and I really believe it was her lying there in the same spot on the sofa she'd always slept in. I was by now feeling euphoric and crying relentlessly! I felt a bit silly, but I didn't care! I knew our dog was back to say hello and that she was no longer in pain. I also believe she was thanking me for sitting with her while the vet gave her the injection. I sat there and talked to her, and told her she didn't need to stay around, and that she could now be free and move on. I don't know why I was talking to my dead dog like that, but I felt it helped her spirit move on.

'When I buried her I placed a toy dog in the grave; the toy had the words "I love you" written on a heart. I guess I just didn't want her to be alone. Since then I have heard her barking at night and she has visited me in dreams (just as you describe in one of your books).

'My mother returned that evening to find us both in a state of shock, with puffy eyes from crying! I told her what had happened and the name my brother said he'd heard and Mum went pale. She showed him a photograph and he went pale, too … it was a picture of my great-grandad, who'd preferred to be called by his middle name, which was Stan, but James was his first name. My brother immediately recognized him as the spirit he'd seen in the front room!

'This was the event that clinched it for me that there is an afterlife. Since then, more interesting things have occurred: I have developed an ability to know when a spirit is in the room because of the emotional changes in energy. I also receive visions, like snapshots of things, people and places.

'I have also realized that there are "signs" in nearly all the photographs of me, even in a picture taken of my mother when she was pregnant with me! There appears to be a man in a silver jacket standing in the way; he's totally obscuring the picture of my mum and other family members. I now consider that to be a sign, and also believe this figure in silver is my spirit guide. I don't know why, it just feels right to me, and it's this feeling of rightness that has helped me to help others contact loved ones, and also help explain phenomena in their homes.

'I've always thought there was "something" everywhere I go, and there is. Spirits are everywhere, and not all of them are pleasant, but it's been my experience that all they need is someone to listen to them and understand. The activity that used to happen in my house has settled down since I've received visions of their favourite places, pictures of their loved ones and, mostly, information on how they died! That was freaky at first and scared me a bit, but now I accept it as normal. The visions are their way of communicating with me.

'Mum and I like to take our new dog to the cemetery where my niece (my mum's granddaughter) is buried. I had a feeling that I needed to go there (that happens to me a lot) but halfway there I had the urge not to go to the graveside, so my mum agreed to turn back, too. As we were walking back up the gravel path I heard a voice say to me, "Tell her it will be OK," so I turned to my mum and said I'd been told to tell her everything will be OK. She questioned me as to what it meant and who'd told me, but I couldn't tell her more as it was all I'd heard.

'My uncle (her brother) was married to a controlling wife who didn't let him see his family or let their children see their grandparents. It was devastating for the family, but the day after we'd been to the cemetery my mum received a phone call from my Nan saying my uncle was leaving his wife and that we would be able to see his children now … I believe that the message I'd had the day before was my spirit guide giving me a sign that the future looked a bit brighter for my family.'

– Steven, England

This next story gave me goosebumps when I read it – it's another one about an angel who protects people from runaway vehicles!

Protected ... Twice

'When I was younger, between the age of 17 months and two years old, I suffered from many fever-based convulsions. One day while I was visiting my grandparents' house I had a convulsion in the spare bedroom, which had been their son's room when he was alive (he died at the age of five).

'From what I have been told by my parents, this convulsion was quite a bad one and I stopped breathing and my lips were blue by the time my parents got to me. My mum began CPR immediately and within a few minutes I came round ... but as I did so I looked up to the ceiling in the bedroom and said, 'Babba gone now' and waved. We believe that the spirit of my mum's brother was watching over me that day.

'My mum also believes that her brother is here as our guardian angel, because when my sister and I were little, we were out shopping with my mum and we were all just about to cross over to the car park when she heard a voice say, "No, cross over there to the left." My mum was bewildered at the time as to why, but she knew she had to obey and so we went a bit out of our way to cross over the road to her left. As we crossed safely, a lorry swerved down the road and ploughed straight into a road sign that was erected in the exact spot where mum had originally been standing. Without a doubt my mum believes that the voice of her guardian angel saved not only her life but mine and my sister's too that day.'

– Gemma, England

Angels don't just come around for life-saving reasons. They can help with everything from passing exams to selling your house ... if you ask them to.

Sold!

'I've been trying to sell my house now for quite a long time. I went to see a friend who suggested I ask angels for help. I did this a few times, but admittedly probably not as enthusiastically as I could have. Then this week I decided to do it again properly. I "contacted" my guardian angel – with amazing results.

'A couple came to view my house last Friday, with a daughter and son who, very strangely, had the same names as my two children. They were also the same number of years apart in age, and currently lived in a house with the same number as ours. I felt so positive after they had been to look round (they were here for almost an hour) that I asked angels again for help selling my house to them. Within half an hour the estate agent called saying that the couple were really interested and wanted to come for a second viewing.

'Well, they came round again the day after, and again I felt really positive about it all. I went out of the room to take a call from the estate agent, and when I came back the TV had changed channels, then a little while later there was a voice (which I couldn't quite make out) coming from my laptop, even though I hadn't opened any different software or websites. I felt that angels were playing with me and making sure I knew they were listening.

'The following day I'd been gardening and was having a well-earned rest in the sunshine when I asked the angels once again for their help. Amazingly, when I opened my eyes I was sure that the "For Sale" sign said "Sold" ... obviously when I looked again it didn't ... not yet, anyway ...

'However, today the family put in an offer and I have accepted it.

'I have to say that this has been one of the most amazing experiences of my whole life, and I will never hesitate to ask the angels for help again.'
– Tracy, England

I know that many readers will be comforted by this next little story. Children are so innocent; they say what they see without question. Have you ever thought about reincarnation? Read on!

Back Again!

'My oldest grandson, James, has amazing psychic sense. He has often displayed his ability to "read minds", and tells women when they are pregnant even when they don't know about it themselves (which can be embarrassing!). He pretty much has been spot-on in each instance.

'He told my middle daughter, when she was expecting her second child, that the baby would be a girl. Everyone else said it was a boy, but he very adamantly said, "No! It's a girl," – and he turned out to be right, much to my daughter's delight.

'On many occasions he's told us that there is someone else in the house, and regularly talks about the "ghosts" he sees. My daughter and I have told him that they are probably angels coming to see that he is OK. He was perfectly happy with all this when he was younger, but at about three to four years of age he started doubting himself.

'One night he was lying in bed with his mum and sister, and he kept hiding under the covers. When my daughter asked him what was wrong, he said that he was scared of the people that were around them. She asked him why and he said that they were very big and that scared him. When my daughter asked him where they were, he pointed to the four corners of the house. He said they were like angels but very, very big. My daughter told him that it was OK because Mama (that's what my grandchildren call me) always asks the angels to guard the house and look after her children and grandchildren by sending the angels to the four corners of their homes for protection. My grandson was very happy with this explanation, and often tells us he can see the angels protecting his home and family.

'The second experience is that my oldest daughter has another boy, Matthew (James' little brother. There are also two sisters). I have always had a kind of "longing affinity" with Matthew, and although I love all of my grandchildren equally, he just melts my heart away. But with him there is a slight difference in the feeling – I couldn't explain it – I don't love him any more than the others, but there is something … When my daughter went to see a psychic (a wonderful lady with a passion for people), she told my daughter that Matthew was the child I had aborted when I was 16 years old. The psychic told her that Matthew just knew he had come into the family at the "wrong" time, first time round, so he'd waited until the time was right and then came back to our family … this time as my grandson. When I heard this, everything seemed to make complete sense to me.

'He is the most amazingly lovable, adorable child, with a calmness and serenity you just couldn't imagine … a real little angel. I have eight grandchildren now and all of them show psychic tendencies. I love them all to bits.'
– Pamela, Australia

If you are interested in more fascinating stories of children's psychic abilities, then look out for my book *Angel Kids*, also published by Hay House.

I couldn't resist adding these next two life-saving stories! How do these things happen: coincidence or angels?

Danger Fall

'I was working for a company in Germany. We constructed printing presses, and part of my duty was to dismantle the walkways and stairs, ready for transport. One day I did a stupid thing and went on the first floor of the press to undo the bolts while holding the checker-plate floor from below. I then went up the stairs to the second floor (about 30–35 feet high) and stood on the plate I had just undone. As I leaned over the edge of the press, it began to tip forwards. I remember falling forward but don't remember what happened after that.

'The next thing I remember is standing on the floor below and hearing the loud crash of the checker-plate floor landing next to me. Somehow I had landed safely on my feet. I was now stood in the only three-foot-square spot with no machine parts in. The co-workers who witnessed my fall began to clap and told me I seemed to know how to come down and land on my feet. They explained that I fell very slowly and the whole thing looked a bit odd. I really started to shake with fright when I realized what had just happened, but besides that I wasn't hurt at all, not even a scratch.

'It's always played on my mind how I was able to fall so slowly and land on my feet. I believe I was guided down by an angel. I still work on printing presses and have never forgotten my experience.'

– Steve, England

This next story is equally puzzling.

Cliff Fall

'When I was nine years old, my friends and I would play in a local quarry quite frequently. It was surrounded by high cliffs and was very deep and extremely dangerous. This one particular day my mam had made me wear this horrible green duffle coat, much to my protests. Later I would be very grateful for that coat!

'I was walking along the cliffs with my friends when all of a sudden I lost my footing and tripped over the side of the cliff. I can remember it vividly, and as I turned over and over I felt every bump and bang. Thank goodness for the thick duffle coat, because it did offer me some protection. Then I remember thinking that I would probably die because once I'd hit the water I would probably drown, especially as the coat was so heavy.

'Suddenly out of nowhere I hit a very thin and small-looking tree. I actually bounced right back onto the stones. My friends came over to me and we all looked at this tree. Where had it come from? None of us remembered it, it hadn't been there before and yet it had literally saved my life.

'The angels were looking down on me that day, I know they were – and I am so grateful to them.'
– Rachel, Wales

Have you ever felt your guardian angel around you? You know you have one, don't you?

Would you like more magical angel experiences in your own life? It's important you ask the angels to help you. Your angels long to be involved in your world – but remember, they aren't allowed to interfere. Invite angels to be a part of your life and I bet you experience more angelic encounters as a result!

If you've had angel experiences of your own, then I'd love to hear from you. You can write to me at the publishers' address (I do read every letter), or if you prefer you can contact me through my website: www.AngelLady.co.uk. I love to read your stories and you too might end up in a book! You can also find me on Facebook and Twitter!

May the angels always be a part of your life.

Jacky x

About the Author

Jacky Newcomb is an award-winning, *Sunday Times* best-selling author, columnist, TV presenter, broadcaster, workshop tutor and speaker. Jacky regularly appears on TV as an expert on angels and the afterlife, on programmes including *This Morning* and *GMTV with Lorraine*.

Jacky is a columnist for *Chat – It's Fate* and *Soul & Spirit* magazines. She writes on a wide range of issues including angels, the afterlife, and paranormal and psychic subjects. Jacky has a special interest in the results of afterlife communication and how it affects healing and grieving in a positive way. Among her clients are grief professionals, doctors and nurses … and celebrities!

Jacky is a regular guest on local and national radio and is frequently interviewed in the national press including the *Daily Mail*, the *Daily Mirror* and the *Daily Express*.

If you want to write to Jacky you can reach her at:

Jacky Newcomb
c/o Hay House Publishers
292b Kensal Road
London W10 5BE

Jacky's websites:
www.AngelLady.co.uk
www.JackyNewcomb.com
www.ThePsychicChildren.co.uk
Jacky is also on Facebook and Twitter

Notes

Notes

Notes

Notes

Notes

Notes

Notes

Notes

Hay House Titles of Related Interest

YOU CAN HEAL YOUR LIFE, the movie,
starring Louise L. Hay & Friends
(available as a 1-DVD set and an expanded 2-DVD set)
Watch the trailer at www.LouiseHayMovie.com

THE SHIFT, the movie, starring Dr Wayne W. Dyer
(available as a 1-DVD program and an expanded 2-DVD set)
Watch the trailer at www.DyerMovie.com

***

Angel Numbers 101, by Doreen Virtue

Ask Your Guides, by Sonia Choquette

Cosmic Ordering for Beginners,
by Barbel Mohr and Clemens Maria Mohr

The Dream Whisperer, by Davina MacKail

The Healing Miracles of Archangel Raphael, by Doreen Virtue

Soul Angels, by Jenny Smedley

Soul Survivor, by Andrea and Bruce Leininger

Angel Therapy Oracle Cards, by Doreen Virtue
How to Give an Angel Card Reading Kit, by Doreen Virtue

***

All of the above are available at your local book shop or may be ordered
by contacting Hay House (see next page).

We hope you enjoyed this Hay House book.
If you would like to receive a free catalogue featuring additional
Hay House books and products, or if you would like information
about the Hay Foundation, please contact:

Hay House UK Ltd
292B Kensal Road • London W10 5BE
Tel: (44) 20 8962 1230; Fax: (44) 20 8962 1239
www.hayhouse.co.uk

***

Published and distributed in the United States of America by:
Hay House, Inc. • PO Box 5100 • Carlsbad, CA 92018-5100
Tel: (1) 760 431 7695 or (1) 800 654 5126;
Fax: (1) 760 431 6948 or (1) 800 650 5115
www.hayhouse.com

***

Published and distributed in Australia by:
Hay House Australia Ltd • 18/36 Ralph Street • Alexandria, NSW 2015
Tel: (61) 2 9669 4299, Fax: (61) 2 9669 4144
www.hayhouse.com.au

***

Published and distributed in the Republic of South Africa by:
Hay House SA (Pty) Ltd • PO Box 990 • Witkoppen 2068
Tel/Fax: (27) 11 467 8904
www.hayhouse.co.za

***

Published and distributed in India by:
Hay House Publishers India • Muskaan Complex • Plot No.3
B-2• Vasant Kunj • New Delhi - 110 070
Tel: (91) 11 41761620; Fax: (91) 11 41761630
www.hayhouse.co.in

***

Distributed in Canada by:
Raincoast • 9050 Shaughnessy St • Vancouver, BC V6P 6E5
Tel: (1) 604 323 7100
Fax: (1) 604 323 2600

***

Sign up via the Hay House UK website to receive the Hay House
online newsletter and stay informed about what's going on with your
favourite authors. You'll receive bimonthly announcements
about discounts and offers, special events, product highlights,
free excerpts, giveaways, and more!
www.hayhouse.co.uk

JOIN THE HAY HOUSE FAMILY

As the leading self-help, mind, body and spirit publisher in the UK, we'd like to welcome you to our family so that you can enjoy all the benefits our website has to offer.

 EXTRACTS from a selection of your favourite author titles

 COMPETITIONS, PRIZES & SPECIAL OFFERS Win extracts, money off, downloads and so much more

 LISTEN to a range of radio interviews and our latest audio publications

 CELEBRATE YOUR BIRTHDAY An inspiring gift will be sent your way

 LATEST NEWS Keep up with the latest news from and about our authors

 ATTEND OUR AUTHOR EVENTS Be the first to hear about our author events

 iPHONE APPS Download your favourite app for your iPhone

 HAY HOUSE INFORMATION Ask us anything, all enquiries answered

join us online at **www.hayhouse.co.uk**

 292B Kensal Road, London W10 5BE
T: 020 8962 1230 E: info@hayhouse.co.uk